FIELD GUIDE

Published by

Please call or write for our free catalog of publications. Our toll-free number to place an order or obtain a free catalog is 800-258-0929 or please use our regular business telephone: 715-445-2214.

Library of Congress Catalog Number: 2002107618
ISBN: 0-87349-528-4

Printed in the United States of America

Contents

(continued next page)

Introduction

The successful hunt for quality antique furniture requires a certain level of familiarity with styles, makers and regional favorites, but whether you're a beginning collector or a seasoned pro, it all comes down to one basic question: Does this piece have any excuses?

By that I mean, is it right in form, function and finish? A piece of furniture that has all three categories—the three "F's"—right will command a higher price, but it also represents a better investment than a piece that offers excuses—or weaknesses—as part of its existence.

As an example, let's look at a popular piece of furniture that comes in myriad styles and see what we can learn.

The "side-by-side" or bookcase desk was a late-19th century invention that offered a compact storage area and writing surface all in one. The basic design is a tall, narrow bookcase with multiple shelves next to a drop-front desk and stacked drawers. Pretty simple at first glance, but the more details we look into, the more we begin to separate the positive attributes from the excuses.

Let's start with wood: Most of these factory-made pieces came in oak, walnut and mahogany, but the choice of wood is not always the most obvious factor in value. A wildly elaborate oak design will still bring more money that a plain, angular piece in walnut or mahogany. Questions to ask: Is the decoration applied or carved into the wood? Is the finish a warm, mellow patina or a stripped-down resurfacing? Is there veneer, and if so, is it flaking and brittle or tight and smooth?

Now more details emerge: Is there a mirror, and is it plain or beveled, square or rounded? Is the glass in the bookcase flat or curved? Is there a shelf or shelves above the desk, and are the supports turned or angular? Is the hardware stamped or cast, and are all the handles original or replacements? Do the hinges appear original or are there phantom holes to show where they've been remounted? Are there storage compartments inside the desk and are they flimsy or solid? Are the drawers nailed together or are they dovetailed? Are the legs straight and plain or carved into scrolls or animal feet?

Finally, is there a maker's name visible, or the label of a retailer to help track its origin? An untouched Gustav Stickley sideboard may look plain and ponderous next to a heavily carved—but anonymous—Victorian-era server with a glossy surface, but the Stickley name is still magic for many collectors.

Country-made pieces in pine, poplar or maple may also have eccentric construction and decoration that appeal to those who favor folksy design, like grain painting, relief carving on the sides, or oddly positioned drawers and shelves.

These are the questions that buyers of antique furniture must keep uppermost in their minds as they decide whether to overlook a piece's excuses, or to keep hunting until all the factors—including the price—are right. This *Warman's Field Guide* provides an excellent starting point as you build your collection. Good luck!

Mark Moran

FURNITURE DATING CHART

AMERICAN FURNITURE

Pilgrim Century – 1620-1700
William & Mary – 1685-1720
Queen Anne – 1720-50
Chippendale – 1750-85
Federal – 1785-1820
Hepplewhite – 1785-1800
Sheraton – 1800-20
Classical (American Empire) – 1815-40
Victorian – 1840-1900
Early Victorian– 1840-50
Gothic Revival – 1840-90
Rococo (Louis XV)– 1845-70
Renaissance Revival – 1860-85
Louis XVI – 1865-75
Eastlake – 1870-95
Jacobean & Turkish Revival – 1870-90
Aesthetic Movement – 1880-1900
Art Nouveau – 1895-1918
Turn-of-the Century
(Early 20th Century) – 1895-1910
Mission-style
(Arts & Crafts movement) – 1900-15
Colonial Revival – 1890-1930
Art Deco – 1925-40
Modernist or Mid-Century – 1945-70

ENGLISH FURNITURE

Jacobean – Mid-17th Century
William & Mary – 1689-1702
Queen Anne – 1702-14
George I – 1714-27
George II – 1727-60
George III – 1760-1820
Regency – 1811-20
George IV – 1820-30
William IV – 1830-37
Victorian – 1837-1901
Edwardian – 1901-10

FRENCH FURNITURE

Louis XV – 1715-74
Louis XVI – 1774-93
Empire – 1804-15
Louis Philippe – 1830-48
Napoleon III
(Second Empire) – 1848-70
Art Nouveau – 1895-1910
Art Deco – 1925-35

GERMANIC FURNITURE

Since the country of Germany did not exist before 1870, furniture from the various Germanic states and the Austro-Hungarian Empire is generally termed simply "Germanic." From the 17th century onward furniture from these regions tended to follow the stylistic trends established in France and England. General terms are used for such early furniture, usually classifying it as "Baroque," "Rococo" or a similar broad stylistic term. Germanic furniture dating from the first half of the 19th century is today usually referred to as Biedermeier, a style closely related to French Empire and English Regency.

Furniture Illustrations & Terms

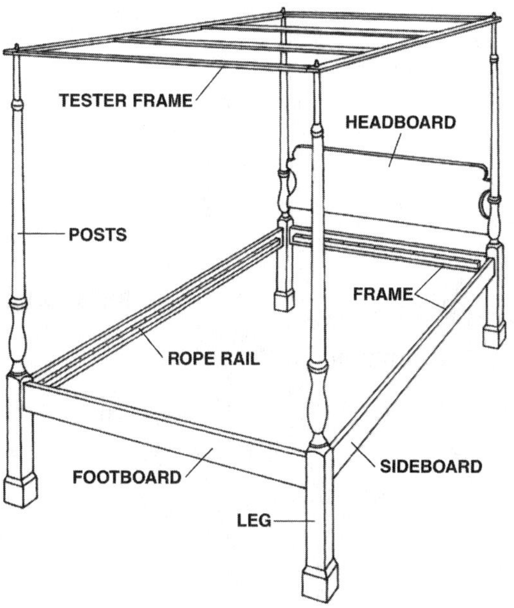

Typical Parts of a Bed

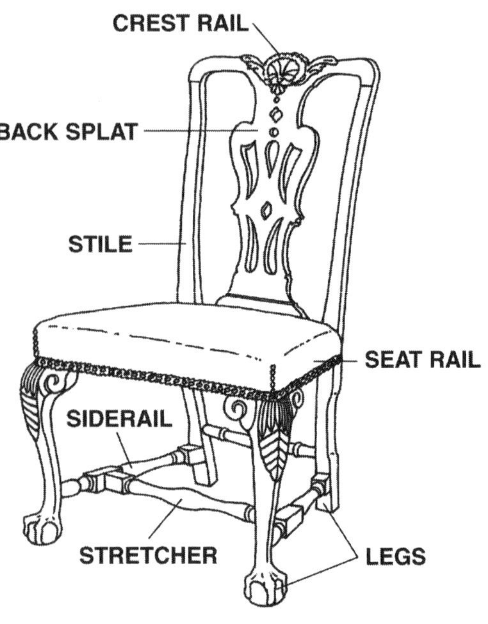

Typical Parts of a Chair

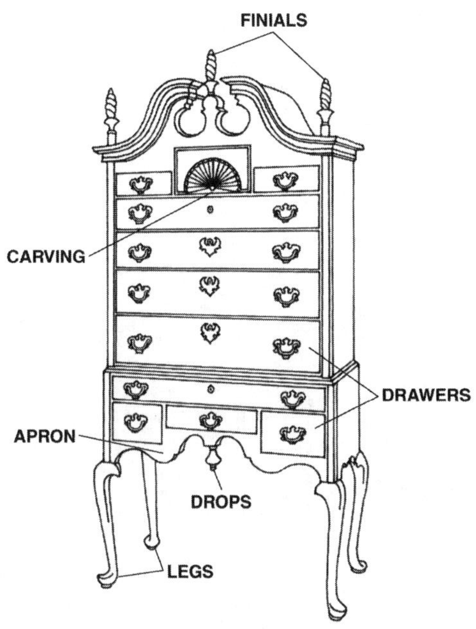

Typical Parts of a Highboy

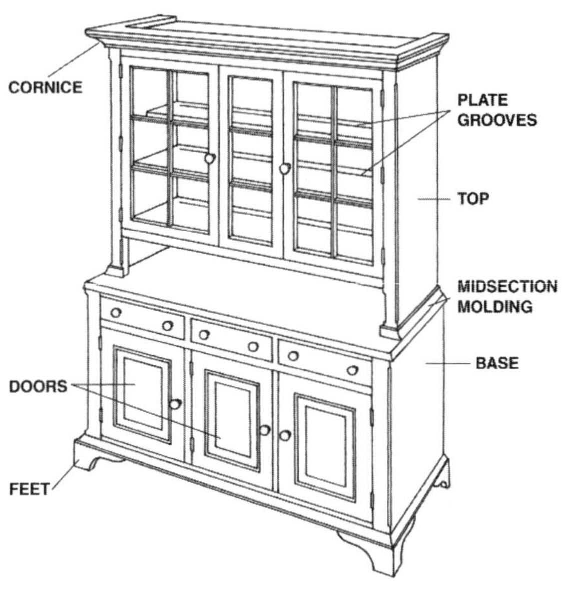

Typical Parts of a Cupboard

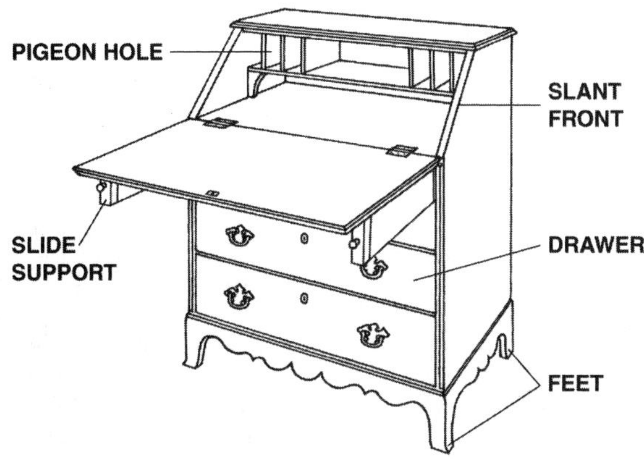

Typical Parts of a Desk

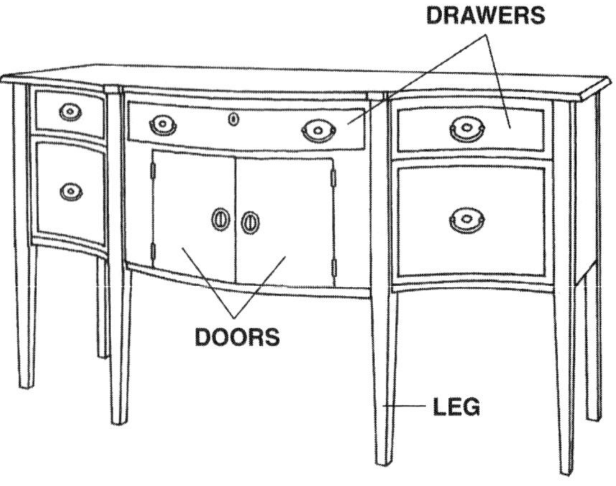

Typical Parts of a Sideboard

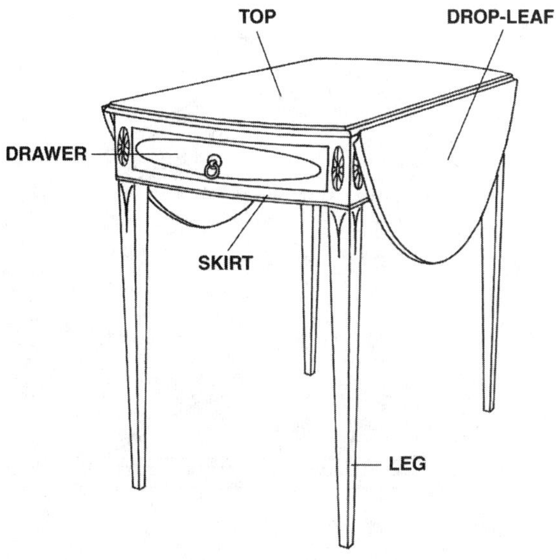

Typical Parts of a Table

Furniture Pediments & Skirts

Classical Pediment

Broken Arch Pediment

Bonnet Top with Urn & Flame Finial

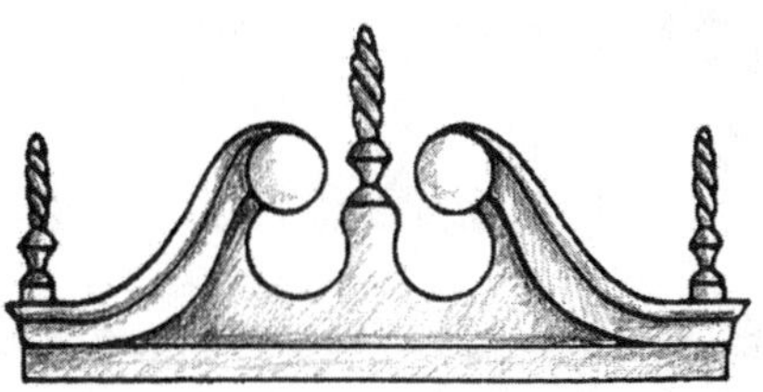

Bonnet Top with Rosettes & Three Urn & Flame Finials

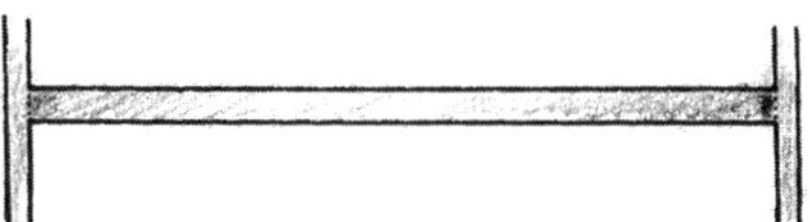

Plain Skirt

Arched Skirt

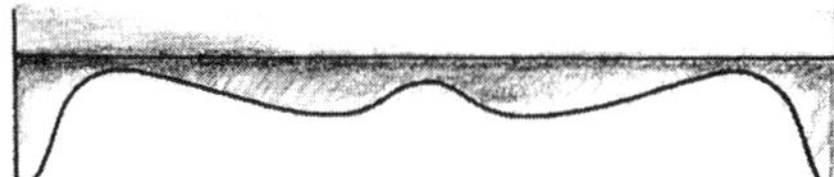

Valanced Skirt

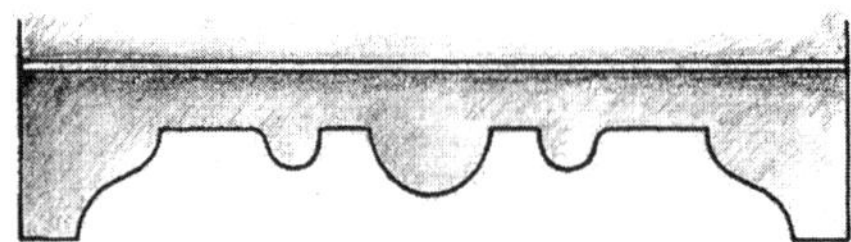

Scalloped Skirt

Furniture Feet

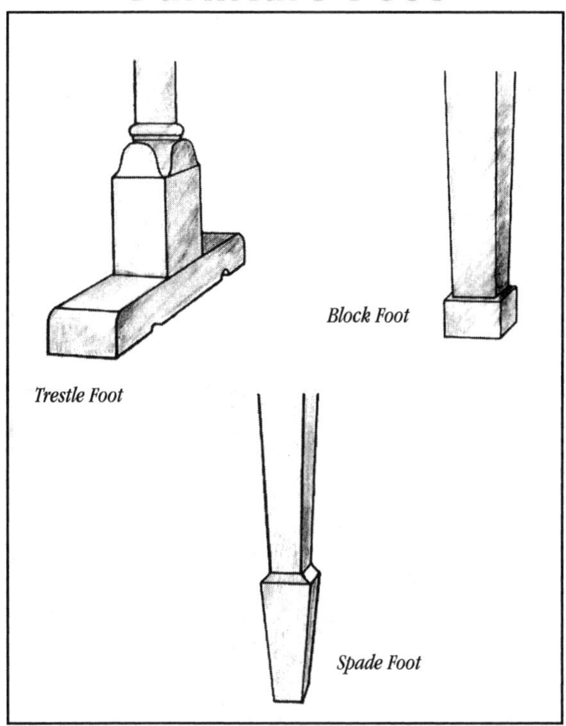

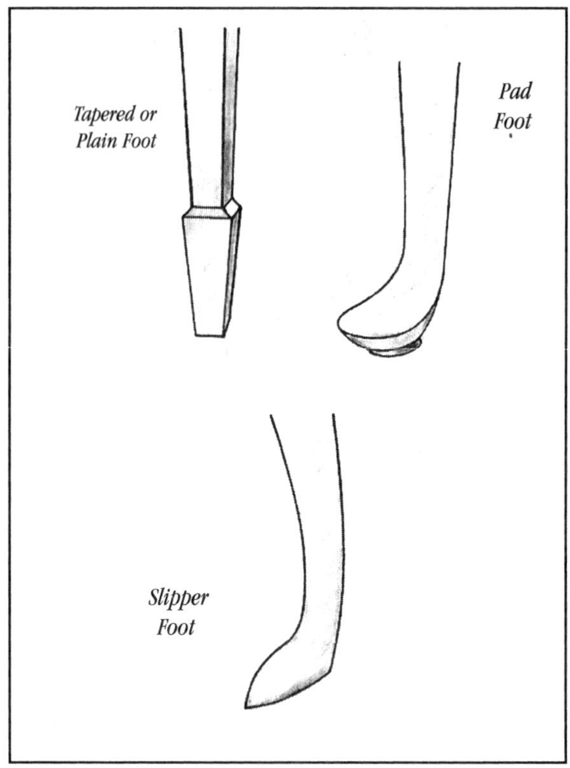
Tapered or
Plain Foot
Pad
Foot
Slipper
Foot

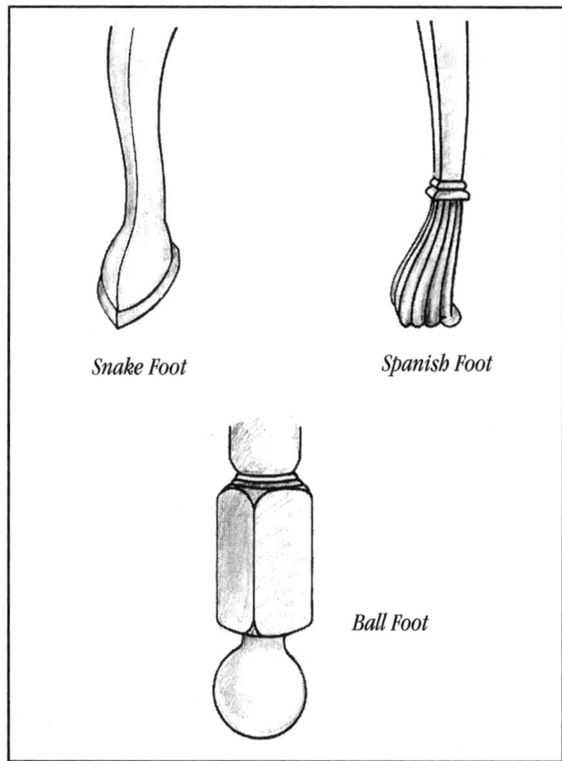

Snake Foot

Spanish Foot

Ball Foot

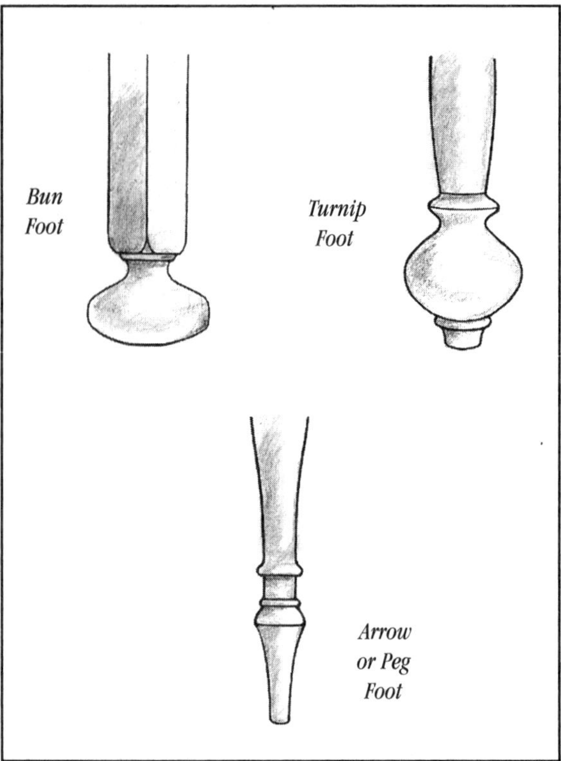
Bun
Foot
Turnip
Foot
Arrow
or Peg
Foot

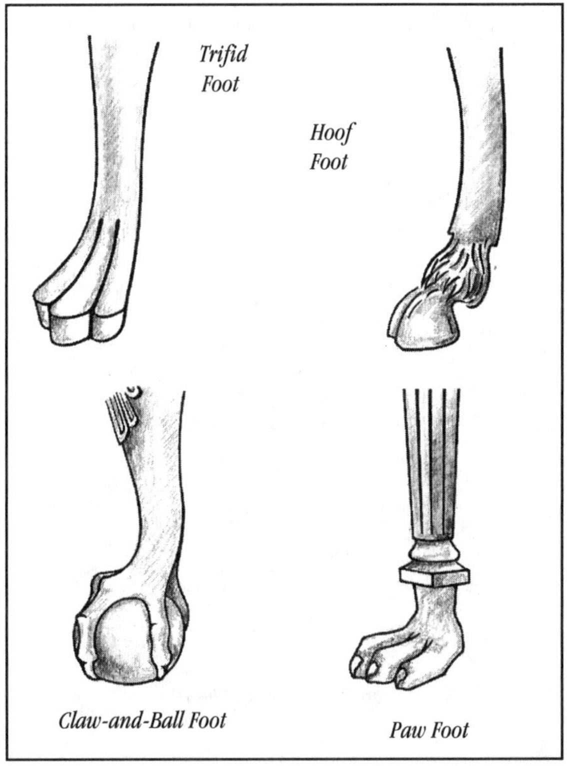
Trifid
Foot
Hoof
Foot
Claw-and-Ball Foot
Paw Foot

Construction Details

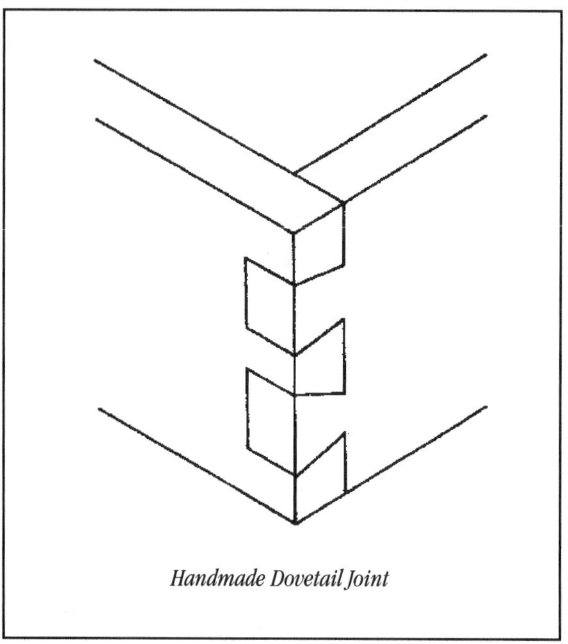

Handmade Dovetail Joint

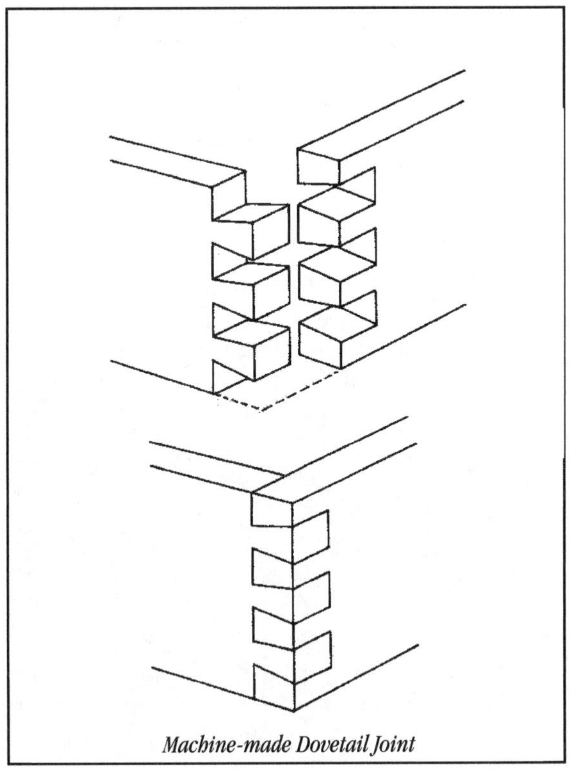

Machine-made Dovetail Joint

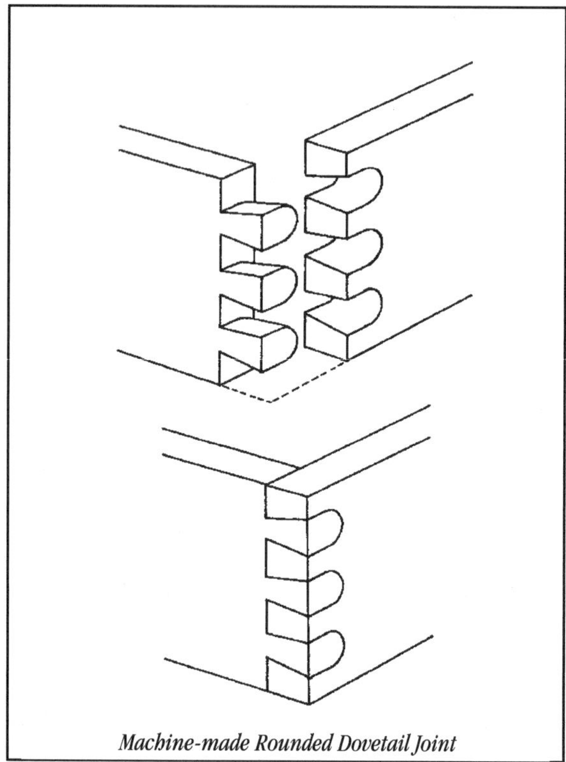

Machine-made Rounded Dovetail Joint

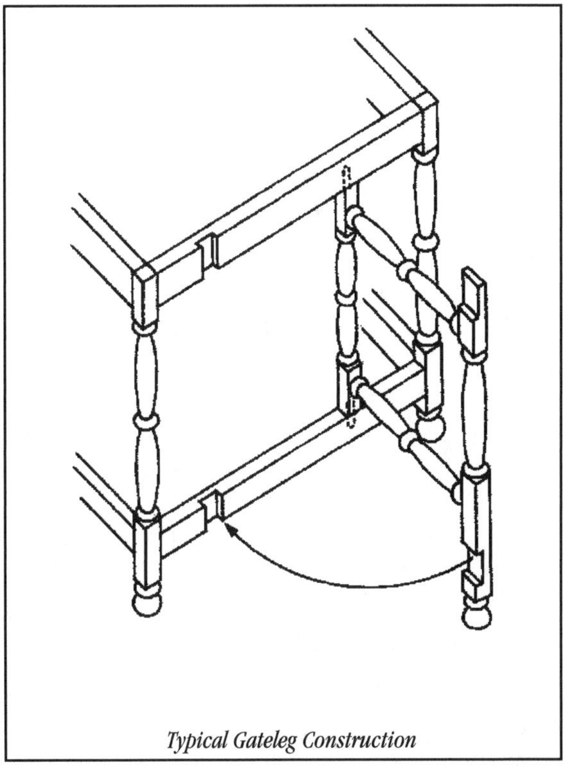

Typical Gateleg Construction

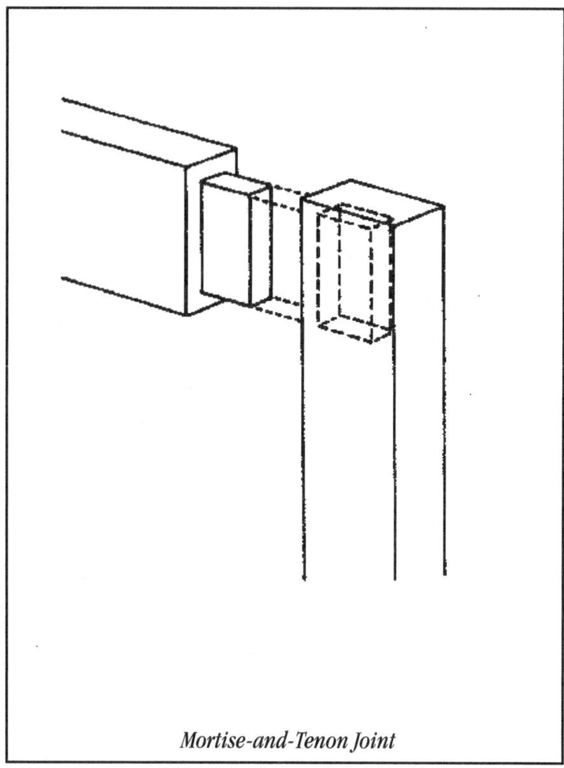

Mortise-and-Tenon Joint

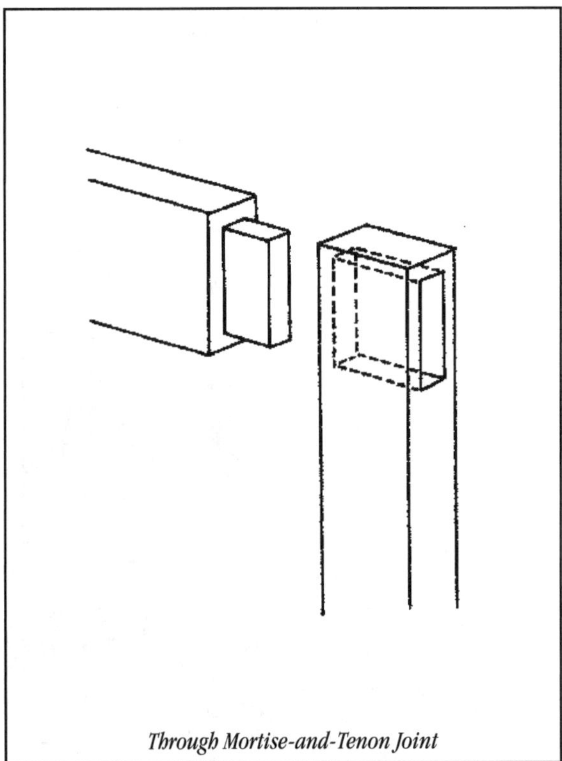

Through Mortise-and-Tenon Joint

Leg Types

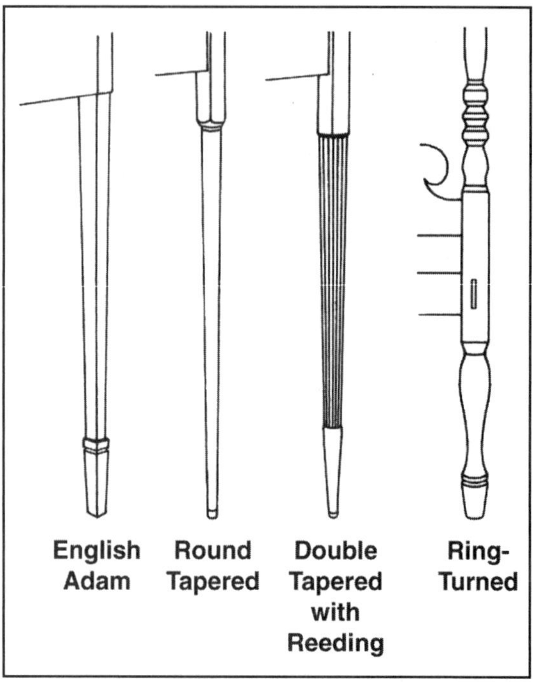
English Adam
Round Tapered
Double Tapered with Reeding
Ring-Turned

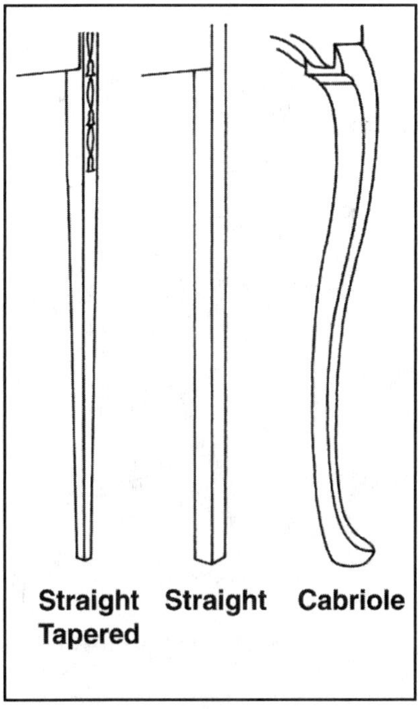
Straight Tapered
Straight
Cabriole

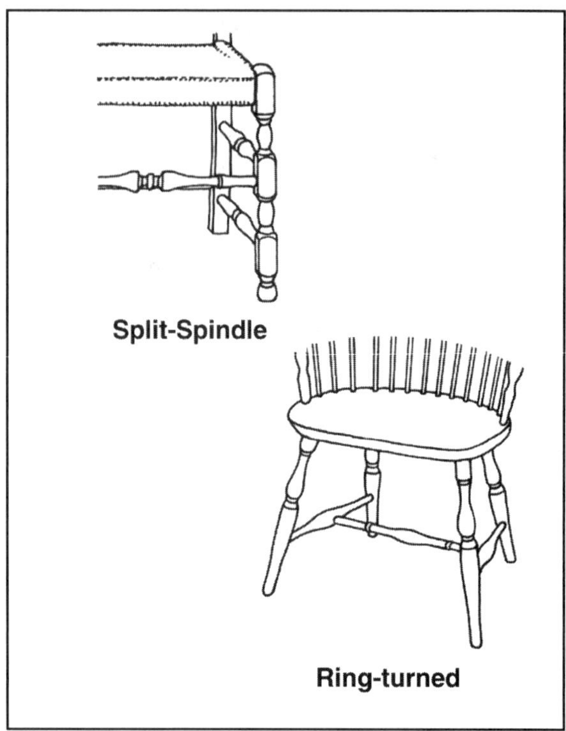
Split-Spindle
Ring-turned

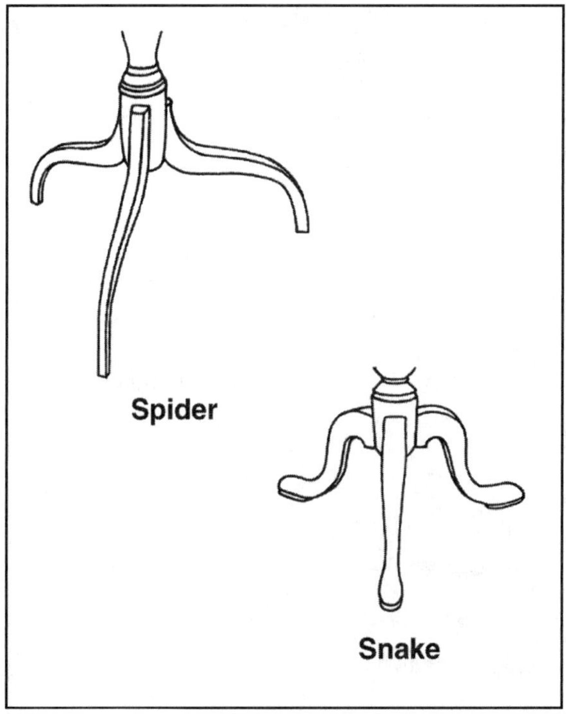
Spider
Snake

Hardware

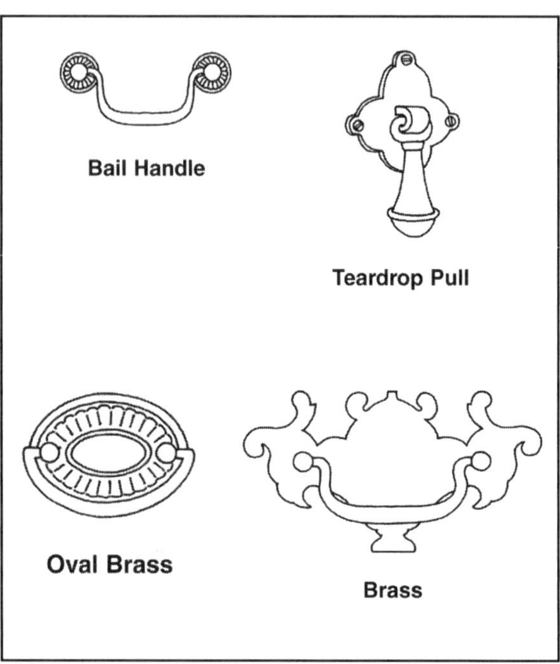

Pressed Glass

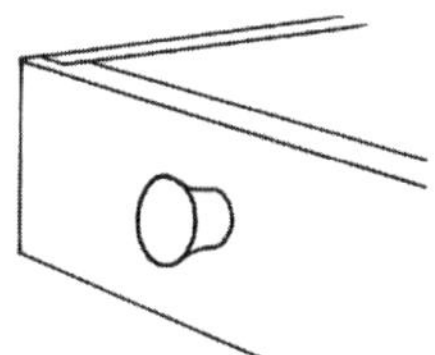

Wooden Knob

Eagle Brass

Furniture Styles

STYLISTIC GUILDELINES: American & English Furniture

AMERICAN

Style: Pilgrim Century

Dating: 1620-1700

Major Wood(s): Oak

General Characteristics:

Case pieces: rectilinear low-relief carved panels, blocky and bulbous turnings, splint-spindle trim

Seating pieces: shallow carved panels, spindle turnings

Style: William & Mary

Dating: 1685-1720

Major Wood(s): Maple and walnut

General Characteristics:

Case pieces: paint decoration, chests on ball feet, chests on frame, chests with two-part construction, trumpet-turned legs, slant-front desks

Seating pieces: molded, carved crestrails, banister backs, cane, rush (leather) seats, baluster, ball and block turnings, ball and Spanish feet

Style: Queen Anne

Dating: 1720-50

Major Wood(s): Walnut

General Characteristics:

Case pieces: mathematical proportions of elements, use of the cyma or S-curve,broken-arch pediments, arched panels, shell carving, star inlay, blocked fronts, cabriole legs and pad feet

Seating pieces: molded yoke-shaped crestrails, solid vase-shaped splats, rush or upholstered seats, cabriole legs, baluster, ring, ball and block-turned stretchers, pad and slipper feet

Style: Chippendale

Dating: 1750-85

Major Wood(s): Mahogany and walnut

General Characteristics:

Case pieces: relief-carved broken-arch pediments, foliate, scroll, shell, fretwork carving, straight, bow, serpentine fronts, carved cabriole legs, claw-and-ball, bracket or ogee feet

Seating pieces: carved, shaped crestrails with out-turned ears, pierced, shaped splats, ladder (ribbon) backs, upholstered seats, scrolled arms, carved cabriole legs or straight (Marlboro) legs, claw-and-ball feet

Style: Federal (Hepplewhite)

Dating: 1785-1800

Major Wood(s): Mahogany and light inlays

General Characteristics:

Case pieces: more delicate rectilinear forms, inlay with eagle and classical motifs, bow, serpentine or tambour fronts, reeded quarter columns at sides, flared bracket feet

Seating pieces: shield backs, upholstered seats, tapered square legs

Style: Federal (Sheraton)

Dating: 1800-20

Major Wood(s): Mahogany and mahogany veneer and maple

General Characteristics:

Case pieces: architectural pediments, acanthus carving, outset (cookie or ovolu) corners and reeded columns, paneled sides, tapered, turned, reeded or spiral turned legs, bow or tambour fronts, mirrors on dressing tables

Seating pieces: rectangular or square backs, slender carved banisters, tapered, turned or reeded legs

Style: Classical (American Empire)

Dating: 1815-40

Major Wood(s): Mahogany and mahogany veneer and rosewood

General Characteristics:

Case pieces: increasingly heavy proportions, pillar and scroll construction, lyre, eagle, Greco-Roman and Egyptian motifs, marble tops, projecting top drawer, large ball feet, tapered fluted feet, or hairy paw feet, brass, ormolu decoration

Seating pieces: high-relief carving, curved backs, out-scrolled arms, ring turnings, sabre legs, curule (scrolled-S) legs, brass-capped feet, casters

Style: Victorian – Early Victorian

Dating: 1840-50

Major Wood(s): Mahogany veneer, black walnut and rosewood

General Characteristics:

Case pieces: Pieces tend to carry over the Classical style with the beginnings of the Rococo substyle, especially in seating pieces.

Style: Victorian – Gothic Revival

Dating: 1840-90

Major Wood(s): Black walnut, mahogany and rosewood

General Characteristics:

Case pieces: architectural motifs, triangular arched pediments, arched panels, marble tops, paneled or molded drawer fronts, cluster columns, bracket feet, block feet, or plinth bases

Seating pieces: tall backs, pierced arabesque backs with trefoils or quatrefoils, spool turning, drop pendants

Style: Victorian – Rococo (Louis XV)

Dating: 1845-70

Major Wood(s): Black walnut, mahogany and rosewood

General Characteristics:

Case pieces: arched carved pediments, high-relief carving, S- and C-scrolls, floral, fruit motifs, busts and cartouches, mirror panels, carved slender cabriole legs, scroll feet, bed room suites (bed, dresser, commode)

Seating pieces: high-relief carved crestrails, balloon-shaped backs, urn-shaped splats, upholstery (tufting), demi-cabriole legs, laminated, pierced and carved construction (Belter & Meeks), parlor suites (sets of chairs, love seats, sofas)

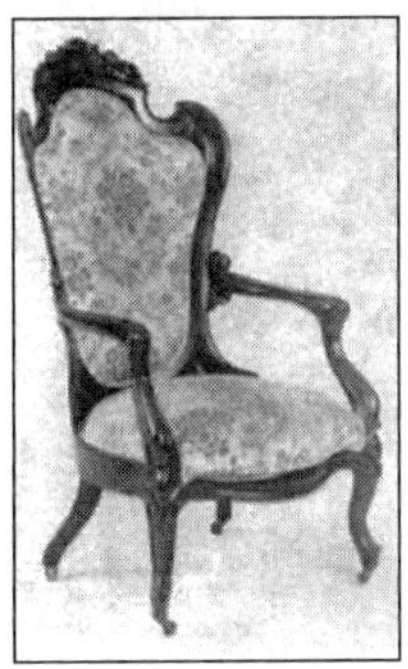

Style: Victorian – Renaissance Revival

Dating: 1860-85

Major Wood(s): Black walnut, burl veneer, painted and grained pine

General Characteristics:

Case pieces: rectilinear arched pediments, arched panels, burl veneer, applied moldings, bracket feet, block feet, plinth bases, medium and high-relief carving, floral and fruit, cartouches, masks and animal heads, cyma-curve brackets, Wooton patent desks

Seating pieces: oval or rectangular backs with floral or figural cresting, upholstery outlined w/brass tacks, padded armrests, tapered, turned front legs, flared, square rear legs

Style: Victorian – Louis XVI

Dating: 1865-75

Major Wood(s): Black walnut and ebonized maple

General Characteristics:

Case pieces: gilt decoration, marquetry, inlay egg & dart carving, tapered turned legs

Seating pieces: molded, slightly arched crestrails, keystone-shaped backs, circular seats, fluted tapered legs

Style: Victorian – Eastlake

Dating: 1870-95

Major Wood(s): Black walnut, burl veneer, cherry and oak

General Characteristics:

Case pieces: flat cornices, stile and rail construction, burl veneer panels, low-relief geometric and floral machine-carving, incised horizontal lines

Seating pieces: rectilinear spindles, tapered, turned legs, trumpet-shaped legs

Style: Victorian – Jacobean and Turkish Revival

Dating: 1870-90

Major Wood(s): Black walnut and maple

General Characteristics:

Case pieces: A revival of some heavy 17th century forms, most commonly in dining room pieces

Seating pieces: Turkish Revival style features: oversized, low forms, overstuffed upholstery, padded arms, short baluster, vase-turned legs, ottomans, circular sofas

Jacobean Revival style features: heavy bold carving, spool and spiral turnings

Style: Victorian – Aesthetic Movement

Dating: 1880-1900

Major Wood(s): Painted hardwoods, black walnut, ebonized finishes

General Characteristics:

Case pieces: rectilinear forms, bamboo turnings, spaced ball turnings, incised stylized geometric and floral, designs, sometimes highlighted with gilt

Seating pieces: bamboo turnings, rectangular backs, patented folding chairs

Style: Art Nouveau

Dating: 1895-1918

Major Wood(s): Ebonized hardwoods, fruitwoods

General Characteristics:

Case pieces: curvilinear shapes, floral marquetry, carved whiplash curves

Seating pieces: elongated forms, relief-carved floral decoration, spindle backs, pierced floral backs, cabriole legs

Style: Turn-of-the-Century (Early 20th Century)

Dating: 1895-1910

Major Wood(s): Golden (quarter-sawn) oak, mahogany, hardwood stained to resemble mahogany

General Characteristics:

Case pieces: rectilinear and bulky forms, applied scroll carving or machine-pressed designs, some Colonial and Classical Revival detailing

Seating pieces: heavy framing or high spindle-trimmed backs, applied carved or machine-pressed back designs, heavy scrolled or slender turned legs, often feature some Colonial Revival or Classical Revival detailing such as claw-and-ball feet

Style: Mission (Arts & Crafts movement)

Dating: 1900-1915

Major Wood(s): Oak

General Characteristics:

Case pieces: rectilinear through-tenon construction, copper decoration, hand-hammered hardware, square legs

Seating pieces: rectangular splats, medial and side stretchers, exposed pegs, corbel supports

Style: Wicker

Dating: mid-19th century-1930

Major Wood(s): Natural woven wicker or synthetic fibers

General Characteristics:

Case and seating pieces: Earlier examples feature tall backs with ornate lacy scrolling designs continuing down to the arms and aprons. Tables and desks often feature hardwood (usually oak) tops. After about 1910 designs were much simpler with plain tightly woven backs, arms and aprons. Pieces were often given a natural finish but painted finishes in white or dark green became popular after 1900.

Style: Colonial Revival

Dating: 1890-1930

Major Wood(s): Oak, walnut and walnut veneer, mahogany veneer

General Characteristics:

Case pieces: forms generally following designs of the 17th, 18th and early 19th centuries. Details for the styles such as William & Mary, Chippendale, Queen Anne, Federal or early Classical were used but often in a simplified or stylized form. Mass-production in the early 20th century flooded the market with pieces that often mixed and matched design details and used a great deal of thin veneering to dress up designs.

Style: Colonial Revial (continued)

Case pieces: dining room and bedroom suites were especially popular

Seating pieces: designs again generally followed early period designs with some mixing of design elements.

Style: Art Deco

Dating: 1925-40

Major Wood(s): Bleached woods, exotic woods, steel & chrome

General Characteristics:

Case pieces: heavy geometric forms

Seating pieces: streamlined, attenuated geometric forms, overstuffed upholstery

Style: Modernist or Mid-Century

Dating: 1945-70

Major Wood(s): Plywood, hardwood or metal frames

General Characteristics: Modernistic designers such as Eames, Vladimir Kagan, George Nelson, and Isamu Nochuchi led the way in post-war design. Carrying on the tradition of Modernist designers of the 1920s and 1930s, they focused on designs for the machine age, which could be mass-produced for the popular market. By the late 1950s many of their pieces were used in commercial office spaces and schools as well as in private homes.

Case pieces: streamlined or curvilinear abstract designs with simple detailing; plain, round or flattened legs and arms commonly used; mixed materials including wood, plywood, metal, glass and molded plastics

Seating pieces: streamlined and abstract curvilinear designs generally using newer materials such as plywood or simple hardwood framing; fabric and synthetics such as vinyl were widely used for upholstery with finer fabrics and real leather featured on more expensive pieces. Seating made of molded plastic shells on metal frames and legs used on many mass-produced designs.

Style: Danish Modern

Dating: 1950-70

Major Wood(s): Teak

General Characteristics:

Case and Seating pieces: This variation of Modernistic post-war design originated in Scandinavia, hence the name. The designs were simple and restrained with case pieces often having simple boxy forms with short rounded tapering legs. Seating pieces have a simple teak frame work with lines coordinating with case pieces. Vinyl or natural fabric was most often used for upholstery. In the United States, dining room suites were the most popular use for this style although some bedroom suites and general seating pieces were available.

ENGLISH

Style: Jacobean

Dating: Mid-17th century

Major Wood(s): Oak, walnut

General Characteristics:

Case pieces: low-relief carving, geometrics and florals, panel, rail and stile construction, applied split balusters

Seating pieces: rectangular backs, carved and pierced crests, spiral turnings ball feet

Style: William & Mary

Dating: 1689-1702

Major Wood(s): Walnut, burl walnut veneer

General Characteristics:

Case pieces: marquetry, veneering, shaped aprons, 6-8 trumpet-form legs, curved flat stretchers

Seating pieces: carved, pierced crests, tall caned backs & seats, trumpet-form legs, Spanish feet

Style: Queen Anne

Dating: 1702-14

Major Wood(s): Walnut, mahogany, veneers

General Characteristics:

Case pieces: cyma curves, broken arch pediments and finial, bracket feet

Seating pieces: carved crestrails, high, rounded backs, solid vase-shaped splats, cabriole legs, pad feet

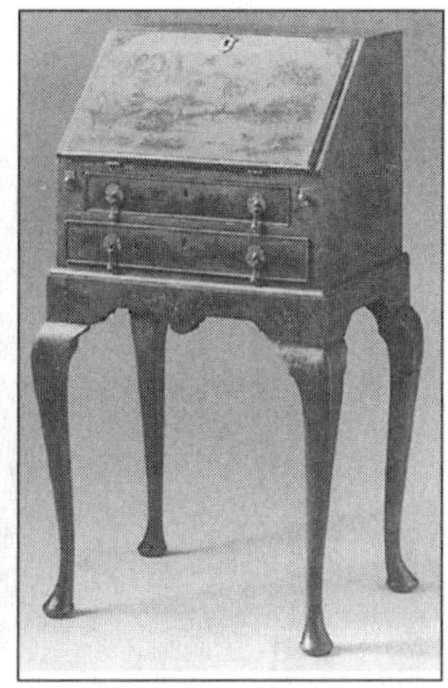

Style: George I

Dating: 1714-27

Major Wood(s): Walnut, mahogany, veneer and yewwood

General Characteristics:

Case pieces: broken arch pediments, gilt decoration, japanning bracket feet

Seating pieces: curvilinear forms, yoke-shaped crests, shaped solid splats, shell carving, upholstered seats, carved cabriole legs, claw-and-ball feet, pad feet

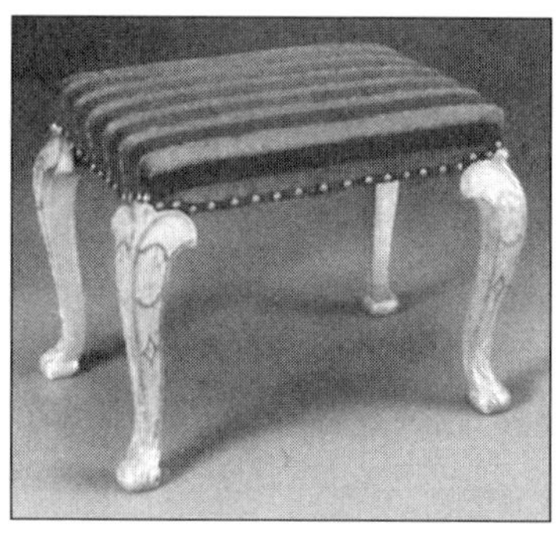

Style: George II

Dating: 1727-60

Major Wood(s): Mahogany

General Characteristics:

Case pieces: broken arch pediments, relief-carved foliate, scroll and shell carving, carved cabriole legs, claw-and-ball feet, bracket feet, ogee bracket feet

Seating pieces: carved, shaped crestrails, out-turned ears, pierced shaped splats, ladder (ribbon) backs, upholstered seats, scrolled arms, carved cabriole legs or straight (Marlboro) legs, claw-and-ball feet

Style: George III

Dating: 1760-1820

Major Wood(s): Mahogany, veneer, satinwood

General Characteristics:

Case pieces: rectilinear forms, parcel gilt decoration, inlaid ovals, circles, banding, or marquetry, carved columns, urns, tambour fronts or bow fronts, plinth bases

Seating pieces: shield backs, upholstered seats, tapered square legs, square legs

Style: Regency

Dating: 1811-20

Major Wood(s): Mahogany, mahogany veneer, satinwood and rosewood

General Characteristics:

Case pieces: Greco-Roman & Egyptian motifs inlay, ormolu mounts, marble tops, round columns, pilasters, mirrored backs, scroll feet

Seating pieces: straight backs, latticework, caned seats, sabre legs, tapered turned legs, flared turned legs, parcel gilt, ebonizing

Style: George IV

Dating: 1820-30

Major Wood(s): Mahogany, mahogany veneer, and rosewood

General Characteristics: Continuation of Regency designs

Style: William IV

Dating: 1830-37

Major Wood(s): Mahogany, mahogany veneer

General Characteristics:

Case pieces: rectilinear brass mounts, grillwork, carved moldings, plinth bases

Seating pieces: rectangular backs, carved straight crestrails, acanthus, animal carving, carved cabriole legs, paw feet

Style: Victorian

Dating: 1837-1901

Major Wood(s): Black walnut, mahogany, veneers, and rosewood

General Characteristics:

Case pieces: applied floral carving, surmounting mirrors, drawers, candle shelves, marble tops

Seating pieces: high-relief carved crestrails, floral & fruit carving, balloon backs, oval backs, upholstered seats, backs, spool, spiral turnings, cabriole legs, fluted tapered legs, scrolled feet

Style: Edwardian

Dating: 1901-10

Major Wood(s): Mahogany, mahogany veneer, and satinwood

General Characteristics: Neo-Classical motifs and revivals of earlier 18th century andearly 19th century styles.

Beds & Bedroom Suites

Art Deco Bedroom Suite

A bed can be found in every household and in every furniture style. Inventories of Colonial estates often listed a bed, but gave much more importance to the bedstead or bed hangings. Why? Because often the early beds were rather plain, and the wealth of the owner was displayed in the elaborate bed hangings used to disguise this fact.

By the Federal period, it was fashionable to have a bedroom on the first floor, primarily to show off one's expensive bed linens and sometimes the more elaborate bed now owned. Beds made for southern climates displayed more carving and details earlier, as

Fine Eastlake Bed & Chest of Drawers

they were less inclined to be draped with heavy bed hangings that were used in colder regions to provide warmth in poorly heated rooms. It was not unusual to find more carving and details lavished on the foot posts since that was what was easily viewed.

Guests were frequently invited into Colonial era bedrooms as a courtesy, perhaps for tea or to socialize. These types of bedrooms were furnished with as fine a piece as the owner could afford, but more emphasis was usually placed on the case pieces used in the room, rather than the bed itself.

Bedroom suites became popular during the Victorian era when furniture was made for every function. By this time, furniture designers were creating beds and accompanying dressers, chests of drawers, chairs, and commodes, as well as matching wash stands. As manufactured furniture became more affordable, larger bedroom suites were created, and it became a sign of prestige to own a fine bed. Victorian era homes and later architectural styles allowed for larger bedrooms often with higher ceilings that could accommodate massive headboards. These masterpieces were made not be covered up with bed hangings, but to be allowed to delight the owner with elaborate carvings, scrolls, and fine woods.

Great architectural changes occurred as the 19th century ended. The Arts & Crafts era, as well as the Mission styles and Art Deco, featured houses with smaller bedrooms, causing furniture designers to create beds and bedroom suites that fit the architectural style. Many of the architects of this era were also furniture designers, creating a complete new environment. One room they often chose to use build-ins and be of a simplified design was the bedroom. Beds returned to rather plain styles, more function than design.

Today new architectural styles are again featuring large bedrooms, often with high ceilings. Modern furniture makers have responded by creating masterful bedroom suites to fill those spaces. Headboards are again soaring and large suites include dressers, chests, matching nightstands, etc. Traditional styles such as Federal and Chippendale are being updated to fit modern mattress sizes and to again display one's wealth by owning a fine bedroom suite.

Gilbert Rhode Bedroom Chests

Art Deco, tall chest of drawers, a chest of drawers w/mirror, a bed & a nightstand; blonde finished hardwood, the tall chest & chest of drawers w/mirror each w/rectangular tops above stacks of long graduated drawers w/catalin pulls, the round mirror supported on a curved tubular metal angled arm, looped tubular metal legs, the bed w/a curvilinear foot-board, round nightstand, signed by designer Gilbert Rhode, manufactured by Herman Miller, Zeeland, Michigan, ca. 1933, tall chest 47" h., the set (ILLUS. of part) **$4,888**

Jacobean Revival, a tall chest of drawers, a dresser w/mirror, a dressing table w/mirror, a double bed, stool & non-matching side chair; mahogany veneer & burled mahogany veneer, the tall chest w/a rectangular top w/molded edges above a long drawer w/a central raised burl panel flanked by carved scrolls & ring pulls w/quarter-round corner turnings above a stepped-back & inset stack of three long burl veneered drawers flanked by ring- and knob-turned outset posts on a rectangular top w/molded edges over a lower case w/two long burl veneered drawers trimmed w/a continuous raised rectangular banding & w/four ring pulls, half-round ring-turned side colonettes above the apron w/double beaded bands centered by a scroll-carved scalloped central section, raised on ring- and double-knob-turned front legs on casters, other pieces w/similar decoration, by the Continental Furniture Company, ca. 1920s, the set **$550**

Louis XV-XVI-Style, double bed, a pair of five-drawer tall side cabinets, a lady's work table, a lady's dressing table, a nightstand, a guerdon, two armchairs, a side chair & footstool; bronze-mounted tulipwood, overall decorated patterned veneered panels w/gilt-bronze mounts in the form of shells, foliage, laurel branches & putto, the bed signed "Linke," France, early 20th c., the footstool associated, the set **$29,500**

Modern style, two single beds, two wardrobes, a nightstand, a dressing table, two benches & a blanket chest; painted beech, the beds & stand w/rectangular frames enclosing vertical slats w/cross-form framing, the two-door wardrobe w/one door composed of slats & the other w/a mirror above a long lower drawer, the dressing table & stool w/slatted base end sections, designed by Bruno Emmel, by A. Siegl, Vienna, early 20th c., the set **$13,800**

Heywood Wakefield Bedroom Suite

Modern style, bed, nightstand, tall chest of drawers & chest of drawers w/mirror; all in a wheat finish, the chests w/rectangular tops w/rounded edges over cases fitted w/five or four long graduated drawers w/central low arched long wood pulls, the shorter dresser fitted at the top w/a large rectangular mirror w/rounded top corners, chests on short rounded feet, matching bed & nightstand, attributed to Heywood Wakefield, ca. 1955, tall chest 46 1/2" h., the set **$978**

Aesthetic Movement Vanity

Victorian Aesthetic Movement, bed, chest of drawers w/mirror, night table, side chair, vanity & side table; ebonized & gilt-decorated, each piece w/a high rounded flat crestrail continuing to form a framework around the mirrored pieces & ornately decorated w/delicate gilt florals, the drawers & panels on each piece also decorated w/delicate gilt fern leaf or floral vine decorations, ca. 1875, the set **$4,600**

Fine Eastlake Half-tester Bed

Victorian Eastlake substyle, a high-back half-tester bed & tall chest of drawers; walnut & burl walnut, the bed w/a rectangular half-tester canopy w/flaring molded cornice above a scallop-cut & scroll-cut front, raised on curved & pierced spindled brackets on the side stiles of the headboard, headboard w/a scroll-carved crown crest above a scroll-carved band & burl panel over narrow burl panel & arch-topped wide lower burl panels, spiral-turned side stiles, the lower footboard w/a gently arched crestrail over scroll carving & a wide burl panel, scroll-cut top corner ears & spiral-turned side stiles, original side rails, refinished, ca. 1880, w/a matching marble-topped chest of drawers, bed 60" w., 10' h., 2 pcs. **$10,500**

Golden Oak Bedroom Suite

Victorian Golden Oak substyle, dresser, double bed & commode; the dresser w/a large rectangular mirror in a frame w/scroll-carved cresting & rounded corners swiveling between turned uprights & a scrolled crestboard above the molded rectangular serpentine top over a conforming case w/a pair of drawers over two long drawers; the matching medium-height headboard w/a large scroll-carved central cartouche, the commode w/a long bowed drawer over two small drawers beside a single paneled door, all on casters, ca. 1890-1900, the set...... **$1,000**

Ornate Moorish Revival Armoire

Victorian Moorish Revival, armoire, single bed & bedside table w/marble top; walnut, burl walnut & parcel-gilt, each piece w/elaborate pierced & carved decoration, the armoire w/an arched & pierced scroll-carved crest above a latticework crestrail between turned corner finials over a plain frieze band on scalloped rounded arched & turned columns above & flanking the set-back paneled doors w/a top rondel, large center panel & ornately parcel-gilt lower panel, a long raised-panel drawer across the bottom, molded base on bun feet, last quarter 19th c., armoire 23 x 51", 76 1/2" h., the set **$4,025**

Renaissance Revival Bedroom Suite

Victorian Renaissance Revival substyle, double bed, chest of drawers w/mirror & wash-stand; walnut & burl walnut, the bed w/a high back topped by a pointed arch shell and scroll-carved crest above a burl panel flanked by rondels & turned corner finials above a wide burl panel flanked by side colonettes above a narrow burl band & corner finials above a plain panel, matching lower footboard, the tall chest w/a similar crest above a long rectangular swiveling mirror above a white marble top over three long drawers, the washstand w/a white marble top w/small shelf above a case w/a long drawer over a pair of doors all trimmed w/burl, ca. 1885, 3 pcs. **$6,700**

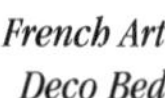

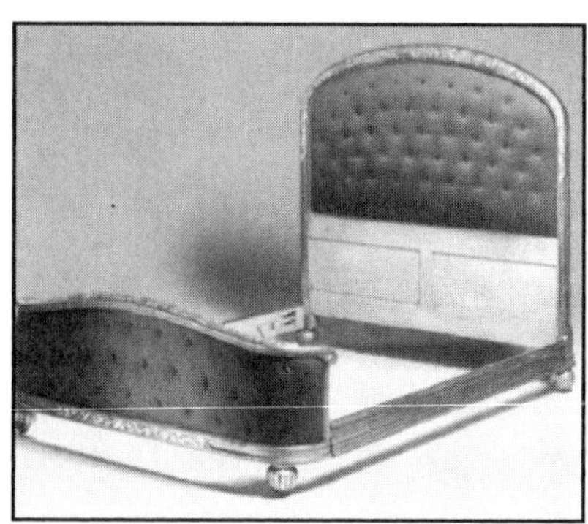

French Art Deco Bed

Art Deco bed, giltwood & upholstery, the high arched headboard & lower footboard carved w/narrow borders of flowerheads enclosing black silk tufted upholstery, joined by molded rails, in the manner of Paul Follot, France, ca. 1925, chips to gilding, 56" w. (ILLUS.) **$2,070**

Art Deco bed, palmwood, the upright thick rectangular headboard joined by low molded siderails continuing into the curved lower footboard on a quarter-round heavy bracket, France, ca. 1930s, veneer losses, 55" w. **$2,875**

Majorelle Art Nouveau Bed

Art Nouveau bed, Les Lilas patt., carved mahogany, the high headboard w/shaped crestrail w/rounded corners over panels of carved lilacs above a wide veneered panel over a rail & four small veneered panels, the conforming lower footboard w/carved corners & two large veneered panels, shaped low feet, designed by Louis Majorelle, France, ca. 1900, 65 x 85", 61" h. **$4,600**

Chippendale Revival Twin Bed

Chippendale Revival style twin beds, mahogany & mahogany veneer, the high headboard w/a broken scroll crest w/carved florettes flanking a central urn & flame finial, tall reeded turned & tapering headposts w/acorn finials, the footboard w/lower matching posts & a serpentined arch top w/gadrooned edging, gadrooned band on footboard rail, headboard w/turned tapering legs w/knob feet, footboard w/claw-and-ball feet, refinished, ca. 1920s, 48" w., 56" h. headboard, pr. (ILLUS. of one) .. **$1,400**

Classical Revival Poster Bed

Classical Revival four-poster bed, mahogany & mahogany veneer, each square corner post topped by ring-turned & leaf-carved sections w/pineapple finials, wide veneered head- and footboard w/round crestrails w/pointed, reeded end finials, short turned tapering legs, original finish & wood casters, three-quarter size, late 19th c., 50" w., 5' 6" h. (ILLUS.) **$1,000**

Classical country-style rope bed, cherry, boldly turned baluster-, ring- and rod-turned head- and footposts w/large ball finials & baluster- and ring-turned legs, the wide headboard w/scrolling crest arched in the center below a turned horizontal rod w/double-ball knobs at each end, the footboard w/a narrow shaped board above the pegged rails, cleaned down to old mellow finish, found in Ohio, first half 19th c., original rails, 51 x 76 1/ 4", 59 3/4" h. **$1,210**

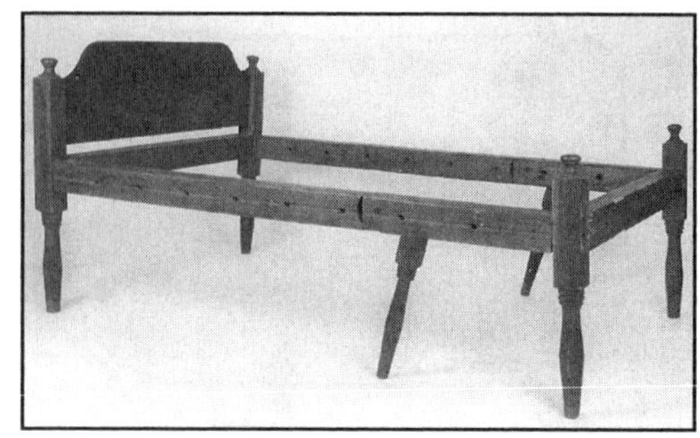

Early Low-poster Rope Bed

Classical sleigh bed, carved mahogany, twin sized, reverse-scrolling head- and footboards on flowerhead- and leaf-carved supports, joined by gadrooned wide side rails on leaf-carved paw feet, New York, first half 19th c. **$5,100**

Country-style low-poster bed, painted, a rounded headboard between square posts w/button finials joined by original hinged side rails to the footposts w/matching finials & joined by a heavy end rail, on ring- and baluster-turned legs w/a pair of fold-down legs where the side rails hinge, original red paint, rails drilled for roping, New England, early 19th c., very minor imperfections, 49 3/4 x 74", 35 1/2" h. (ILLUS.) **$805**

Massachusetts Federal Bed

Federal tall-poster bed, carved mahogany, the square tapering tall headposts centering a scroll-cut pine headboard, the footposts w/waterleaf-carved tapering reeded posts on swag- and leaf-carved urn-form supports on square tapering legs, all legs w/spade feet, w/flat tester, headboard possibly replaced, North Shore Massachusetts, ca. 1795, 59 x 80", 92" h. (ILLUS.) **$5,750**

Federal tall-poster bed, carved mahogany, the vase- and ring-turned footposts carved w/pineapples above a reeded swelled post w/carved sheaves of wheat continuing to acanthus leaves & carved palmettes on vase- and ring-turned legs, the headposts also vase- and ring-turned but uncarved, all joined by a flat tester frame, 54 x 72", 87" h. **$12,650**

Federal-Style Child's Bed

Federal-Style child's tall-poster tester bed, maple, the arched canopy frame w/small center urn finial raised on a tester frame on tall slender tapering corner posts of the high spindle-sided rails, raised on baluster- and ring-turned tapering legs on casters, original finish, ca. 1920s, 24 x 48", 5' h. (ILLUS.) **$800**

Federal tall-poster tester bed, mahogany veneer, the mahogany veneered flat tester w/central rectangular tablets & ovolo corners above spiral- and leaf-carved footposts & turned red-painted headposts flanking a scrolled headboard, ring- and knob-turned legs, Salem Massachusetts, early 19th c., 52 x 76 1/2", 89" h. (some old refinish & height loss) **$4,888**

Gustav Stickley Bed

Mission Style (Arts & Crafts movement) double bed, the headboard & slightly shorter footboard each w/a narrow inverted V-top crestrail flanked by tall square tapering posts, five wide slats in each w/a wide lower rail, original finish, branded signature mark of Gustav Stickley, original side rails, 59 x 78" (ILLUS.) **$8,800**

Mission Style (Arts & Crafts movement) double bed, oak, tall square corner posts, the headboard w/rails flanking the seven slats, matching but slightly lower footboard, wide side rails, fine original finish, L. & J.G. Stickley, Model No. 84, 58" w., 54" h. **$7,150**

George Nelson "Thin Edge" Bed

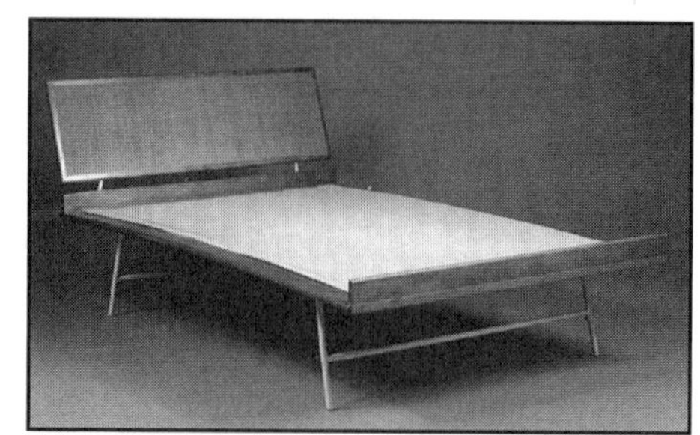

Modern style "Thin Edge bed," walnut, the wood frame w/an upright canted caned headboard, resting on a white-painted tubular steel frame & legs, metal tag marked "Herman Miller - George Nelson Design," ca. 1959, 58 x 82 1/4", 33 1/2" h. (ILLUS.) **$8,740**

Turn-of-the-century brass bed, the high headboard w/a straight bar crestrail joined to ring-turned tall cylindrical stiles w/ball caps & pointed ring-turned finials, the headboard composed of a latticework of ball- and ring-turned vertical & horizontal bars centered by a panel w/a large C-form cartouche, matching lower footboard, on casters, polished, 55 x 72", 67 1/2" h. (one finial missing) **$2,200**

Victorian Golden Oak Double Bed

Victorian Golden Oak bed, the high headboard w/a scroll- and shell-carved center crest above a leaf-carved frieze band flanked by carved ears over rectangular panels, the lower footboard w/a heavy rounded crestrail over a wide panel, refinished, ca. 1910, full size, headboard 72" h. **$800**

Tall Renaissance Revival Bed

Victorian Renaissance Revival bed, walnut & burl walnut, tall-back style, the very tall headboard w/an arched & molded pediment crest centered by a tall leaf- and scroll- carved finial & scroll & burl panel trim above projecting blocks over slender turned columns & shaped sides flanking a tall raised panel flanked by shorter side panels w/corner blocks w/turned finials, the lower footboard w/a flat top rail over rectangular, round & arched raised burl panels, canted blocked corners w/turned columns, old refinish, ca. 1875, 58" w., 8' h. **$3,500**

Fine Victorian Rococo Bed

Victorian Rococo, mahogany & mahogany veneer tall-poster style, monumental round headposts w/squatty flame-turned finials above the high arched headboard w/a shell- and fruit-carved crest over scrolled borders & two raised triangular panels above a large inset rectangular panel w/a rosette at each corner, gadrooned turning at the base of each post, the low footboard w/short round posts w/pointed gadrooned caps & bands above long Gothic arch panels flanking the low arched & scroll-carved footrail w/a central rosette & oval banding, old dark finish, some reconstruction, minor veneer damage, orig-inal rails, ca. 1850, 63" w., headposts 101" h. **$6,875**

Benches

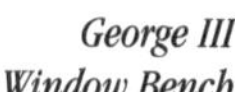

George III Window Bench

Benches represent a form of furniture with many functions. Some benches were made for seating purposes, such as a church pew or window seat. Others were made to assist in the daily living tasks, such as a water bench, designed to hold buckets of water. Benches usually display the same furniture design elements as chairs or tables. Style identification is often attributed by either knowing the original function of the bench or studying the feet or arms.

As furniture styles became more upholstered, benches became settees and sofas, giving the user more comfort. While architectural styles often dictated furniture design, benches and chairs are good examples of how clothing styles affected furniture form. Large wide skirts, full of padding and underlayers didn't require as much padding on a piece of furniture. As clothing styles became sleeker, padding was added to benches in the form of cushions and pillows.

Art Deco Bench

Art Deco bench, mahogany, the reeded curved backrail continuing to half arms above an upholstered oblong seat w/fluted apron raised on square tapering & slightly curved legs joined by an H-stretcher, ca. 1930, 17 x 35 1/2", 21" h. (ILLUS.) **$1,680**

Bench, painted pine, the overhanging rectangular seat on shaped supports & arched cut-out feet joined by a straight skirt, vestiges of original salmon paint, probably Pennsylvania, ca. 1840, 11 3/4 x 77 3/4", 19 3/4" h. .... **$ 2,760**

Bucket (or water) bench, country-style, painted, a superstructure w/a narrow shelf w/a high three-quarters gallery above a row of three small drawers w/cast-iron finger pulls, shaped tapering tall sides above the wide rectangular lower shelf over a case w/a pair of paneled cupboard doors w/cast-iron thumb latches, slender bracket feet, old yellow repaint over earlier colors, pulls overpainted, 19th c., 17 1/4 x 42", 48" h. .. **$4,400**

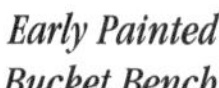
Early Painted Bucket Bench

Bucket (or water) bench, painted pine, a rectangular top w/chamfered edges above an apron w/a pair of drawers w/turned wood knobs above two long open shelves, bootjack ends, old surface w/remains of old red paint, possibly New England, early 19th c., minor imperfections, 18 x 55 1/2", 40" h. (ILLUS.) **$4,025**

Bucket (or water) bench, country-style, poplar, the tall superstructure w/a rectangular top above a closed back w/a single shelf above a projecting rectangular well above a long deep dovetailed drawer above the closed back & lower shelf, one-board ends, worn red finish, 19th c., 21 3/4 x 42", 59 1/2" h. (some edge damage, feet worn down & w/some dry rot) **$2,420**

Golden Oak Hall Bench

Bucket (or water) bench, painted wood, the shallow shelf above a projecting lower shelf joined by cut-out sides & double-arch cut-out feet, probably New England, early 19th c., 10 1/2 x 28", 26" h. (imperfections) **$3,738**

Cobbler's bench, pine, rectangular top w/a large square lid over a compartment at one end beside three small compartments w/sliding lids over shallower wells & above a row of small square drawers w/wood knobs along the bottom of the case, raised on slightly outset slender square tapering legs, w/a shoe pattern cut out from a newspaper dated 1829, old refinish, 14 x 36", 20" h. **$1,815**

Country-style bench, painted poplar, mortised construction, long narrow board top above narrow beaded aprons w/shaped ends, wide shaped bootjack legs, green repaint & scrubbed top, 19th c., 13 1/2 x 39", 18 1/2" h. (age cracks) **$358**

George Nelson Modern Style Bench

Country-style bench, stained pine, long narrow rectangular top above narrow rounded side aprons & bootjack ends, square nail construction, embossed "C--an.Dom" on end, 19th c., 9 x 31 1/2", 8" h. (one later nail added) **$495**

Kneeling bench, painted wood, narrow long top on low base, grey-painted graining on a putty-colored ground, 19th c., 6 x 28 3/4", 7 1/2" h. (wear) **$1,840**

Kneeling bench, poplar, a long narrow board top w/a narrow apron raised on three arched bootjack legs, old brown finish, 7 x 76 3/4" **$220**

Kneeling bench, walnut, a narrow long rectangular top above a rounded-end apron, on short bootjack legs mortised through the top, old patina, late 19th c., 5 1/2 x 36" **$275**

Hall bench, Victorian Golden Oak substyle, a wide crestrail w/a serpentine top edge above long carved scrolls over a row of five slender turned spindles, flat back stiles w/curved ears above the shaped open arms on incurved arm supports flanking the rectangular lift-lid seat over a deep well, simple cabriole legs, refinished, ca. 1900, 16 x 30", 32" h. (ILLUS. on previous page) **$450**

Modern-style bench, a rectangular long seat composed of solid maple slats raised on three ebonized wood trapezoidal open legs, designed by George Nelson, produced by Herman Miller, ca. 1956, 72" l., 14" h. (ILLUS.) **$1,568**

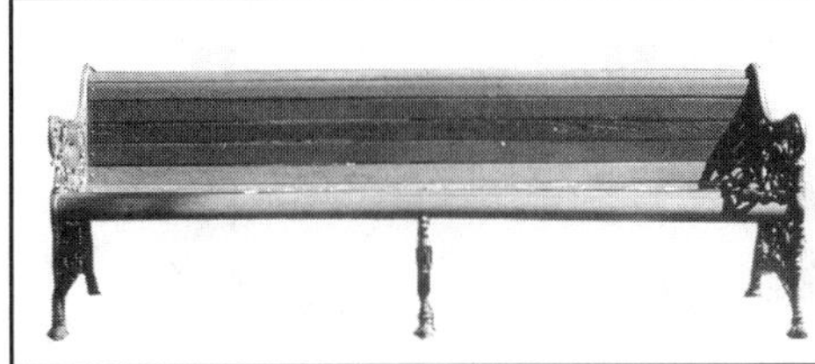

Long Wood & Iron Park Bench

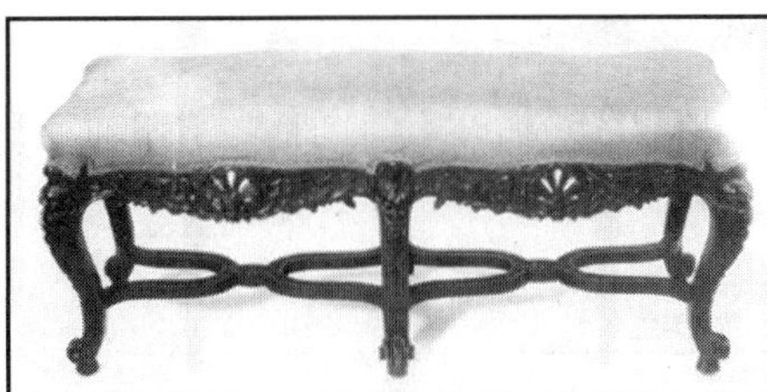

Regency-Style Bench

Park bench, cast-iron & wood, the long wooden slat back & seat joining the pierced scrolled iron arms above pierced ends of squirrels among leafy vines on short legs of gargoyles ending in paw feet, painted green, George Smith and Co., Glasgow, Scotland, late 19th c. 31 x 98", 33" h. (ILLUS.) **$2,070**

Regency-Style bench, walnut, a long serpentine-edged upholstered top in green striped silk over a foliage-carved & shell-pierced apron, raised on six cabriole legs ending in scrolled toes, joined by stretchers, Europe, late 19th c., 17 x 45 1/2", 17" h. (ILLUS.) **$1,840**

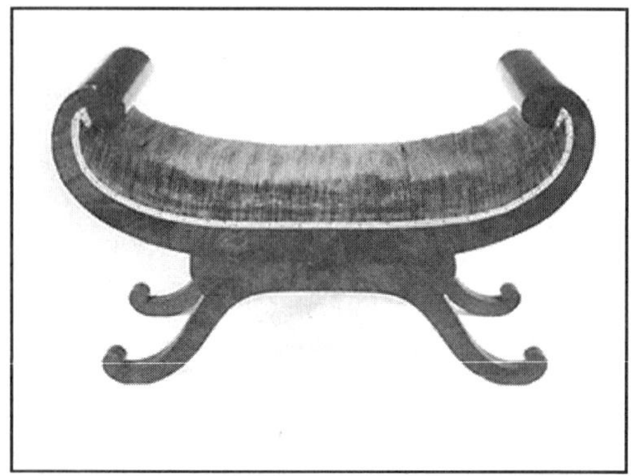

Classical Window Bench

Window bench, Classical style, mahogany veneer, the up-curving seat flanked by scrolled ends above four outscrolled legs, New York, 1815-25, old refinish, some veneer cracking & loss, 14 x 39 1/2", 23 5/8" h. **$3,450**

Window bench, upholstered mahogany, the long upholstered rectangular seat w/raised rolled end arms, raised on six square molded legs joined by stretchers, on casters, George III era, England, late 18th c., 18 3/4 x 51", 26" h. **$6,900**

Bookcases

Breakfront Renaissance Bookcase

Bookcases are shelved units, often with doors to enclose the shelves. Interiors may have movable or fixed shelving. Because many bookcases are built into rooms, finding an authentic free-standing bookcase from early periods is difficult.

The barrister bookcase is a common name for the stacking bookcase popularized in the Victorian era. These can be found in various combinations, some with molded tops, others with drawers in the bases. Several different manufacturers made this type of bookcase.

Arts & Crafts, Gustuv Stickley Bookcase

As with other large pieces of furniture, look for wear in places where doors open and where hands might have rested while looking for a favorite book. Check to see that doors open easily, that all mechanical parts are present and in good working condition. It is not too unusual to find a pane of glass or two replaced over the lifetime of a well-used bookcase.

Also see Secretaries.

English Arts & Crafts Bookcase

Arts & Crafts bookcase, oak & leaded glass, a rectangular top w/molded edges above a frieze band & narrow molding over a pair of tall glazed cupboard doors w/upper panels of geometrically-glazed panels of striated green & colorless glass, opening to four wooden shelves, molded apron w/rounded block front feet on casters, England, late 19th c., wear, 14 1/4 x 40", 58 1/4" h. **$805**

Cherry Chippendale Bookcase

Chippendale bookcase, cherry, the flat rectangular top w/a flared cornice above a pair of large 12-pane glazed cupboard doors w/molded muntins opening to four shelves above a pair of long thumb-molded drawers w/replaced butterfly brasses, molded base on scroll-cut ogee bracket feet, old refinish, New England, ca. 1790, restored, 13 x 58 1/2", 62 1/2" h. **$4,313**

Fine Classical Mahogany Bookcase

Classical bookcase, parcel-gilt mahogany & mahogany veneer, two-part construction: the upper section w/a rectangular top over a wide flattened flaring cornice over a deep veneered frieze band above a pair of glazed cupboard doors flanked by large carved parcel-gilt scrolls at the top & base sides above a row of three small round-fronted drawers; the lower section w/a projecting rectangular top above a long arched frieze drawer, raised on heavy scrolled legs carved at the front w/acanthus leaf, the sides w/grapevines & ending in large paw feet, above an incurved lower shelf raised on foliate-carved toupie feet, possibly Philadelphia, ca. 1830, 22 1/2" x 43", 5' 11 1/2" h. .. **$9,200**

Unusual Oak Stacking Bookcase

Early 20th century bookcase, quarter-sawn oak, four-section stacking lawyers-type, the rectangular top w/a flared rounded cornice above the top section w/a leaded glass lift-front door above two matching sections w/plain glass lift-front doors set on the stepped-out bottom section w/a large glass lift-front door on a flat rounded base rail, refinished, ca. 1910, 18" x 32", 4' 10" h. **$1,200**

Fine Federal Bookcase

Federal bookcase, inlaid mahogany, two-part construction: the upper section w/a rectangular top & molded swans-neck crest w/openwork foliate designs centering a turned urn finial on a plinth inlaid w/oval foliage above a cove-molded cornice w/geometric band inlay over a frieze band & a pair of tall geometrically glazed cupboard doors w/incurved inlaid muntins centered by églomisé rectangular portrait medallions of George & Martha Washington, signed "by Kennedy, Balt.," the lower case w/a rectangular top over four long beaded graduated drawers w/string inlay over an inlaid band & scalloped apron continuing to tall French feet, the bookcase section w/a lift-top secret compartment behind the cornice, ca. 1800, 38 1/4" w., 88" h. **$9,775**

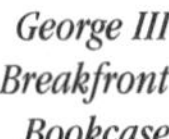

George III Breakfront Bookcase

George III bookcase, mahogany, two-part breakfront-type: the upper section w/a removable paterae-mounted cornice above four tall multi-paned glazed doors w/Gothic arch-top panes opening to three shelves; the lower section w/mid-molding & conforming stepped-out central section w/a pair of paneled cupboard doors flanked by paneled end doors opening to shelves, on low bracket feet, England, ca. 1800, 19 x 77", 86" h. **$10,350**

Georgian-Style Mahogany Bookcase

Georgian-Style bookcase, mahogany, three-door design, a rectangular top above a Chinese trellis-carved frieze band above the three tall glazed doors w/serpentine edged glazed panels over short matching blind panels, flanked by canted front corners w/garland-carved bands above reeded bands, molded base on scroll-cut bracket feet, England, ca. 1920, 18 x 72", 5' 4" h. **$2,000**

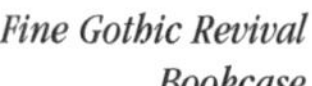
Fine Gothic Revival Bookcase

Gothic Revival bookcase, mahogany & mahogany veneer, the rectangular top w/rounded front corners on the deep coved cornice above a pair of tall glazed doors w/arched mullions at the top, opening to four shelves, on a shaped bracket base, ca. 1840, 15 x 52", 83" h. **$5,700**

Mission-style (Arts & Crafts movement) bookcase, oak, a rectangular top w/three-quarters gallery w/through-tenons above a pair of tall 8-pane glazed doors opening to shelves, flat base

L. & J.G. Stickley Mission Bookcase

w/through-tenons, hammered copper pulls, labeled "The Work of L. & J.G. Stickley," Model No. 643, ca. 1912, 12 1/8" x 36 1/2", 55 1/2" h. (ILLUS.) **$6,900**

Mission-style (Arts & Crafts movement) bookcase, oak, rectangular case w/overhanging top above double doors each w/eight small square leaded glass panes over pairs of tall narrow panes, flanked by a column w/capital at each side, above an arched apron, designed by Harvey Ellis, partial Craftsman paper label of Gustav Stickley, Model No. 73, ca. 1904, 14 1/8" x 54", 58" h. **$15,525**

Aesthetic Movement Oak Bookcase

Victorian Aesthetic Movement bookcase, quarter-sawn oak, the rectangular top w/a low three-quarters gallery centered by a low arched crest carved w/acorns & oak leaves above a square central paneled door carved w/a spray of oak leaves & acorns flanked by open side compartments backed by rectangular beveled mirrors & arched framing w/ring- and baluster-turned corner supports above a case w/three tall glazed cupboard doors opening to three shelves, a row of three drawers w/stamped brass pulls across the bottom, molded base on casters, refinished, ca. 1895, 18" x 60", 6' h. (ILLUS.) **$3,500**

Mission-style (Arts & Crafts movement) bookcase, oak, a rectangular narrow top w/a low galleried top w/keyed tenon ends above a case w/three tall 12-pane glazed cupboard doors opening to shelves, flat apron, lower keyed tenons & low arched end openings, original hammered copper hardware, fine original finish, Handcraft decal mark, L. & J.G. Stickley, Model No. 647, 12" x 73", 55" h. **$17,600**

Fine Baroque Revival Bookcase

Victorian Baroque Revival bookcase, mahogany & mahogany veneer, the rectangular top w/a narrow beaded flared cornice above a wide frieze band ornately carved w/leafy scrolls above a pair of wide single pane glazed doors flanked by reeded slender pilasters, two ornately scroll-carved drawers at the bottom w/lion head pulls, molded base raised on large paw feet on casters, refinished, ca. 1890, 18" x 50", 5' h. **$2,800**

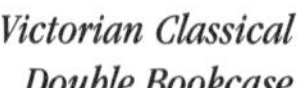

Victorian Classical Double Bookcase

Victorian Classical bookcase, walnut, the rectangular top w/a deep coved cornice above a pair of tall 4-pane glazed doors w/pierced scroll-carved top corner brackets opening to adjustable shelves over the stepped-out base w/a pair of drawers w/black pear-shaped drop pulls, deep flat molded base, refinished, ca. 1850-70, 20" x 48", 6' 8" h. **$1,800**

Victorian Country-style Tall Bookcase

Victorian country-style bookcase, walnut, the rectangular top w/a deep stepped & flaring cornice above a pair of 4-pane arch-topped doors w/solid lower panels opening to five adjustable shelves, the stepped-out lower section w/a single long paneled drawer w/ wood knob pulls, slightly scalloped apron & simple bracket feet, demountable, refinished, ca. 1850, 18" x 45", 7' h. **$2,500**

Fine Golden Oak Double Bookcase

Victorian Golden Oak bookcase, quarter-sawn oak, a long low crestrail w/rounded ends above the rectangular top w/narrow carved frieze band above a long open compartment w/spindled end panels & two long narrow beveled mirrors above a scroll-carved band over a pair of tall glazed cupboard doors opening to two adjustable shelves, deep molded base on thin square feet, refinished, ca. 1900, 18 x 60", 68" h. (ILLUS.) **$3,300**

Victorian Renaissance Revival bookcase, walnut & burl walnut, two-part construction: the top section w/a rectangular top w/a flaring stepped cornice above a paneled frieze band w/burl panels & a center roundel above a pair of tall arched glazed doors w/triangular burl panels at the top corners & flanked by leaf-carved drops & raised burl panels down the sides, opening to three shelves; the lower stepped-out section w/a pair of deep

Renaissance Revival Bookcase

drawers w/long shaped raised burl panels & black pear-shaped pulls flanked by burl panels, deep molded plinth base, ca. 1875, 20 x 42", 64" h. (ILLUS.) **$2,000**

Victorian Renaissance Revival bookcase, walnut & burl walnut, breakfront style, the tall central projecting section w/a high crest topped by a broken-scroll crestrail centered by a high carved flame-form finial above deep molding over an arched panel centered by a large relief-carved bust of a woman w/a floral wreath in her hair all above a tall arched glazed door opening to adjustable shelves, the lower side cabinets w/broken-scroll crests on molded flaring cornices above burl frieze panels over the arched glazed cupboard doors opening to adjustable shelves, three drawers across the base each w/a raised burl panel & pairs of brass loop & bar pulls, deep molded flat base, refinished, ca. 1870, 22 x 72", 8' 5" h. **$9,000**

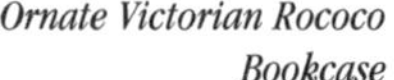

Ornate Victorian Rococo Bookcase

Victorian Rococo bookcase, carved rosewood, two-part construction: the upper section w/an arched top w/a high ornate pierced, scroll-carved crest above a floral-carved frieze band & blocked corners above a pair of tall glazed arched doors w/delicate scroll-carved edging flanked by outset corner blocks w/bold leaf-, scroll- and floral carving & w/a pair of narrow drawers just below the doors; the stepped-out lower section w/conforming blocked corners & a pair of narrow drawers w/oval banding above a pair of paneled cupboard doors w/delicate scroll-trimmed edging, molded serpentine apron, leaf- and scroll-carved blocked front corners above compressed bulbous feet, ca. 1850-60, 25 x 52", 95" h. **$4,140**

Late Victorian Oak Bookcase

Victorian turn-of-the-century bookcase, oak, a rectangular top w/a narrow flared cornice above a tall case w/a pair of large glazed doors w/inset rectangular panels at the bottom above a deep molded flat base, beaded board pine back, opens to five adjustable shelves, short section of molding missing at the side, ca. 1900, 18 x 68", 83" h. **$1,045**

Cabinets

Oak Side-by-Side China Cabinet

Cabinets of all shapes and sizes have been created through all styles of American furniture. Many were designed to accommodate a specific social function, while others were designed for storage purposes.

As with other forms of furniture, today's collectors of American furniture enjoy the history of why a piece was created, but many choose to use their cabinets for a slightly different reason. Because many cabinets are small, they easily fit into many room settings.

Classical Revival Music Cabinet

Cabinets are different than stands or tables in that they have a door or doors to access storage areas.

Comments about design elements relating to a particular style are not included, as it often is difficult to determine by the cabinet style. Many times usage, types of materials used, or other clues are more beneficial to determining age.

• China cabinets appeared on the decorating scene when it became important to display one's wealth by displaying the finest china. Originally designated for dining rooms, china cabinets were often part of dining room suites. Some china cabinets were made to complement existing future styles and blend in nicely. Today collectors often feature china cabinets in other rooms to house their collections of all types of things. Another common name for a china cabinet is china closet. Expect to find grooved plate rails in many of the shelves of china cabinets to facilitate horizontal display of china plates.

• Before the advent of steel filing cabinets, those who designed offices created wooden filing cabinets to help take care of the clutter of business and get it organized.

• Just as maps and prints deserve their own special storage cabinet, so does sheet music.

• Side cabinets are small cabinets used by the side of a chair, sofa, or perhaps in a bedroom.

• Spool cabinets were designed for the display of multicolored thread on store countertops. Collectors today enjoy their wide drawers for a variety of uses. Most spool cabinets have either two or four drawers. The better the advertising and the better the original condition, the higher the value.

• Like china cabinets, display cabinets are meant to display a collection or things that indicate the owner is wealthy or possesses good taste. Another name for display cabinet is "vitrine." Many furniture designers created display cabinets to be included in living room or den settings. Many vitrine cabinets are lighted to further enhance their contents. If modifying an antique display cabinet with lighting, take into consideration what the heat and light rays will do to your objects.

Small Art Deco China Cabinet

China cabinet, Art Deco style, burl walnut veneer, a stepped & triple-arched top above a conforming case w/a pair of 2-pane tall glazed central doors opening to two long glass shelves flanked by two glazed side panels, on a deep serpentine apron, electrified, ca. 1930s, 11 1/4 x 44 1/2", 50" h. **$546**

Unique Arts & Crafts China Cabinet

China cabinet, Arts & Crafts style, oak, the rectangular top w/an upright stepped & paneled crestboard w/metal mounts above a case w/a pair of glazed cupboard doors w/a pair of small panes flanking a central pane overlaid w/a pierced stylized spearpoint copper ornament above two tall narrow panes all above a pair of small square paneled doors flanking a stack of four small drawers at the bottom, long spearpoint copper strap hinges & inset pulls, matching glazed sides, short stile legs joined by sleigh feet on casters, metal tag marked "From Alexander H. Revel & Co. Chicago, Ill.," Model No. 8646, Stickley Brothers, ca. 1908, 18 x 48", 75 1/4" h. **$14,100**

China Cabinet with Carved Lion Heads

China cabinet, late Victorian, oak, the half-round top w/outset front corners above curved glass sides & a curved glass door w/carved lion heads topping the front framework, pair of stylized cabriole legs in the front & simple curved legs at the rear, ca. 1900 .... **$1,600**

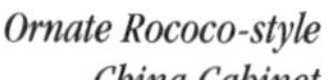

Ornate Rococo-style China Cabinet

China cabinet, late Victorian Rococo-style, mahogany, the half-round case w/a high wide arched molded crestrail centered by a high scroll-carved crest above a tall arched glazed cupboard door flanked by curved glass sides all enclosing three glass shelves, conforming base w/scroll-carved apron, on short front cabriole legs w/claw-and-ball feet.................................. **$9,000**

Harvey Ellis-Designed Cabinet

China cabinet, Mission-style (Arts & Crafts movement), oak, a rectangular top overhanging a case w/a tall glazed cupboard door w/an arched top rail & a metal plate & ring pull, arched apron, designed by Harvey Ellis, produced by Gustav Stickley, ca. 1904, 15 1/4 x 36", 60" h. **$8,625**

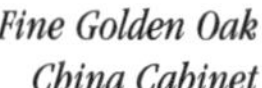
Fine Golden Oak China Cabinet

China cabinet, Victorian Golden Oak, the half-round top w/a high pointed & ornately scroll-carved crest above a pair of projecting tall reeded columns dividing the curved front glass door from the curved glass sides, molded conforming base raised on front paw feet on casters, encloses four wooden shelves w/a mirrored back at the top shelf, refinished, ca. 1895, 20 x 44", 70" h. **$3,400**

Chippendale Revival Curio Cabinet

Curio cabinet, Chippendale Revival style, mahogany, two-part construction: the very tall upper section w/a broken-scroll pediment w/pierced lattice carving & a small central platform finial above a cornice w/a dentil molding over a lattice-carved frieze band above the very tall geometrically-glazed cupboard doors opening to shelves; the stepped-out lower section w/a rectangular top w/molded edge above a long deep drawer w/lattice-carved border banding flanked by lattice-carved side stiles, narrow serpentine apron raised on slender carved cabriole legs ending in scroll feet on pegs, original finish, ca. 1890s, 20 x 34", 7' 6" h. **$1,800**

Delicate Louis XV-Style Curio Cabinet

Curio cabinet, Louis XV-Style, walnut, two-part construction: the upper section w/an arched & scroll-trimmed cornice above a three-section case w/tall slender side doors w/tall oblong mirrors w/scrolled borders above a rounded scroll reserve flanking the slightly outset central cabinet section w/a glazed door w/delicate scrolling wood overlay opening to three shelves; the stepped-out lower section w/a pierced lattice & scroll-carved apron raised on four slender & gently backswept cabriole legs joined at the base w/an arched & scrolled X-stretcher, France, late 19th - early 20th c., 16 x 43", 75" h. **$2,475**

Early 20th Century Filing Cabinet

Filing cabinet, early 20th century, oak, a rectangular flat top above a stack of four deep square drawers w/brass rectangular name tag holders & simple curved pulls, flat base, refinished, ca. 1900-20, 16 1/2 x 25", 51 1/2" h. **$358**

Mission Oak Gun Cabinet

Gun cabinet, Mission-style (Arts & Crafts movement), oak, a rectangular top w/a high three-quarters gallery above a tall 2-pane glazed door w/metal pull opening to a rack for rifles above a single drawer at the bottom, arched front apron, original finish & key, brass tag marked "Yeager Gun Cabinet - Allentown Pa - USA.," 14 x 23", 70 1/2" h. (ILLUS.) **$1,650**

Hanging wall cabinet, Victorian Aesthetic Movement substyle, cherry, the crestrail flanked by pointed end crests above a narrow shelf over a small cabinet w/a beveled glass door w/a cut-out top band flanked by open side shelves w/slender columns supporting the ends of the upper shelf, the right side of cabinet shelf extended & w/a low scroll-cut back, the lower section below the cabinet w/a paneled back-board w/scalloped rim, original finish, ca. 1890m 8 x 26", 24" h. (small glued edge break) **$440**

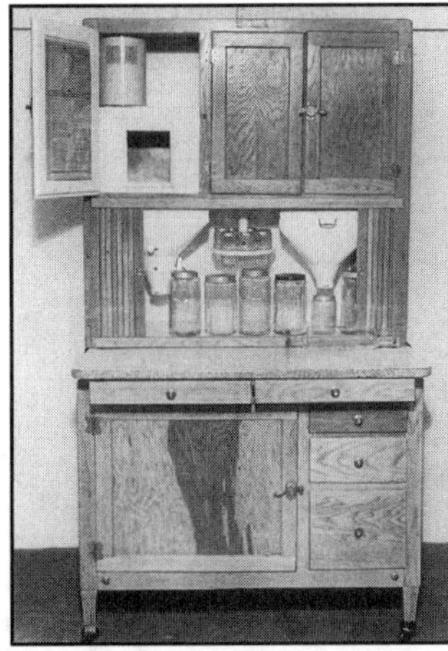

Early Labeled Hoosier Cabinet

Kitchen cabinet, early 20th century Hoosier-style, oak, the superstructure w/a rectangular top above a pair of paneled cupboard doors beside a wide door opening to a bin compartment above a high tambour-front storage area w/metal funnel-form bins flanking a hanging spice rack above a row of storage jars, the lower section w/a rectangular white porcelain-covered metal work surface above a pair of thin pull-out work shelves above a wide rectangular door beside a stack of three graduated drawers, square tapering legs on casters, original paper door inserts, repairs & strips of wood in tambour doors reinstalled, marked "Hoosier," ca. 1900, 22 x 41", 72" h. **$825**

Classical Revival Music Cabinet

Music cabinet, Classical Revival style, mahogany veneer, a rounded crestrail w/a scroll-carved center finial above the rectangular top over a case w/a round-fronted veneered drawer w/round brass pulls & a brass keyhole escutcheon above a flat paneled door w/fine crotch-grained veneering & a brass knob, gadrooned base band, raised on short cabriole legs ending in carved paw feet, refinished, ca. 1910, 14 x 22", 42" h. **$650**

Gustav Stickley Music Cabinet

Music cabinet, Mission-style (Arts & Crafts movement), oak, a rectangular top w/a stepped three-quarters gallery above a tall narrow paneled door w/a rectangular plate & ring pull, flat apron, branded mark of Gustav Stickley, Model No. 70w, ca. 1912, 16 x 20", 46" h. **$7,475**

Louis XV-Style Curio-Music Cabinet

Music & curio cabinet, Louis XV-Style, Vernis Martin finish, a rectangular glass top w/serpentine front banded w/brass above a conforming case, a low mirror-backed curio display section w/glass on three sides & trimmed w/brass banding above a medial brass band above a single wide door centered by a rectangular allegorical painted panel w/brass banding & a scalloped apron, brass-banded side panels, raised on simple cabriole legs w/brass mounts, early 20th c., 15 x 20", 36" h. **$750**

Art Deco Side Cabinet

Sewing cabinet, Mission-style (Arts & Crafts movement), oak, a square top flanked by wide drop leaves above the deep apron w/a stack of two short drawers w/original copper ring pulls, square stile legs, cleaned original finish, some restoration to the top, unsigned Gustav Stickley, Model No. 630, 18" sq., 28" h. **$1,210**

Side cabinet, Art Deco, chrome-mounted rosewood & burlwood, a narrow stepped rectangular black marble top w/wide central section w/a pair of flat cupboard doors in light wood flanked by graduated stacks of four drawers each, all on a high plinth base, repairs, losses to veneer, France, ca. 1930, 19 1/2 x 58", 39 1/2" h. (ILLUS.) **$2,070**

Decorated Arts & Crafts Cabinet

Side cabinet, Arts & Crafts style, oak, a rectangular top above a paneled long door w/a wooden latch & pyrographic picture of a peasant woman carrying a basket, each side trimmed w/three narrow slats, door opens to single shelf, square stile legs project at top corners, early 20th c., minor wear, 13 3/4 x 19 1/2", 42 1/2" h. **$978**

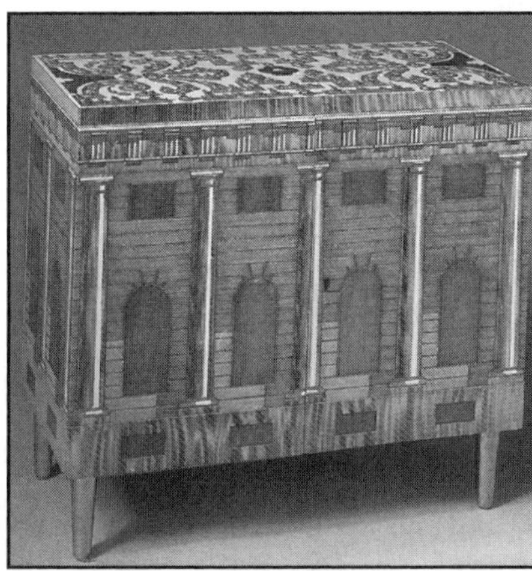

Modern Style Fornasetti Cabinet

Side cabinet, Modern style, transfer-printed decoration, rectangular top w/a black & white printed copy of scrolls & figured designs above a case covered w/a continuous print of a building w/a classical facade, two doors in the case, on tapering brass legs, Piero Fornasetti design, ca. 1950s, 13 3/4 x 27 1/2", 24 3/4" h. **$5,175**

Napoleon III Decorated Side Cabinet

Side cabinet, Napoleon III, gilt-bronze mounted marquetry-inlaid, a rectangular top w/outset rounded corners & a slightly outset central section above a conforming frieze band w/gilt classical banded designs above a conforming case w/the central cupboard door painted w/a panel depicting 18th-century lovers in a landscape, some damages, France, late 19th c., 17 x 52", 42 1/2" h. **$3,220**

Neoclassical Revival Side Cabinet

Side cabinet, Neoclassical Revival style, painted wood, a tall flat rectangular superstructure w/upper painted rectangular panel of 17th c. figures in a landscape above a large nearly square mirror bordered by molded bow & leafy vines flanked by tall slender panels w/molded clusters of trophies at the top & a classical urn at the bottom, all above the rectangular top w/molded edge above a cupboard w/a pair of flat flush cupboard doors painted w/a continuous oval landscape reserve w/delicate leafy scrolls above & below & flanked by narrow painted side panels, on short square legs, pale green ground w/gilt & polychrome painting, France, superstructure 19th c., base 20th c., wear, edge damage & paint touch-up, 12 x 48", 94 1/2" h. **$1,650**

Gothic Revival Side Cabinet

Side cabinet, Victorian Gothic Revival substyle, a rectangular white marble top w/molded edges & rounded corners above a frieze w/a pair of narrow drawers framed by Gothic arch molding above a pair of cupboard doors also w/Gothic arch molding, scalloped apron & bracket feet on casters, marble top may be of later date, stenciled mark in drawers, C.A. Baudouine, New York City, ca. 1840, 21 x 45", 36 1/2" h. **$3,300**

Renaissance Revival Side Cabinet

Side cabinet, Victorian Renaissance Revival substyle, walnut, marquetry & parcel-gilt, the angular shaped top w/a removable statuary stand above an incised frieze band over a central cabinet door w/swag-framed & molded panel decorated w/an ornate floral & ribbon marquetry design flanked by reeded pilasters & angled side panels, all on a molded flaring conforming base w/shaped feet, ca. 1880, minor damage, 22 x 50 1/4", 51 3/4" h. **$3,738**

Victorian Rococo Side Cabinet

Side cabinet, Victorian Rococo substyle, carved rosewood, a white marble D-form top w/serpentine front edge above a conforming case w/a stack of four serpentine molded & fruit-carved drawers w/turned wood knobs flanked by quarter-round top drawers over quarter-round side cabinet doors w/large boldly carved fruit & nut clusters, conforming scroll- and cartouche-carved apron, New York City, ca. 1850-60, 21 x 52", 37 1/2" h. **$2,530**

Silver Cabinet, Baroque Revival style, figured walnut veneer, the arched top w/a small medallion crest over the molded crestrail above the case w/a wide center door w/an upper arched & glazed panel w/scrolling grillwork over a veneered panel flanked

Fine Baroque Revival Silver Cabinet

by narrow side panels inset w/oval glass panes w/cut starburst designs, the lower section w/a deep mid-molding over a case w/a single wide, deep drawer w/three arched panels in the front trimmed w/burl, burl banding & scrolls & w/brass teardrop pulls, raised & carved vertical dividers, a molded carved bottom molding w/a carved center drop raised on four legs w/bulbous reeded & gadrooned turnings above an incurved medial shelf on bun feet, original dark finish, ca. 1930, 20 x 42", 6' 4" h. **$950**

Fine Clark's Walnut Spool Cabinet

Smoker's cabinet, Mission-style (Arts & Crafts movement), oak, overhanging rectangular top above a single drawer & cabinet w/an arched apron, red decal mark of Gustav Stickley, Model No. 89, ca. 1910, 15 x 20 1/8", 29" h. **$3,450**

Speciman cabinet, Federal style, mahogany, a rectangular top above a case w/two stacks of nine long narrow cockbeaded drawers fitted w/a locking mechanism & flanked by reeded stiles, on short tapering turned legs w/knob feet, Philadelphia, ca. 1815, 22 x 42 1/2", 38 1/2" h. (shrinkage cracks, top warpage) **$9,775**

Spool cabinet, walnut, rectangular top w/molded edges above a case w/six long narrow drawers w/teardrop pulls, each w/a red etched-glass panel w/wording, flat molded base, panels read "Clark's - Spool Cotton - O.N.T. - Sole Agent - George A. Clark - On White Spools," refinished, late 19th c., 16 x 22", 20" h. (ILLUS.) **$2,200**

Outstanding Louis XV-Style Vitrine

Vitrine cabinet, Louis XV-Style, gilt-bronze mounted abalone & inlaid wood, two-part construction: the top section w/a high curved & arched cornice fitted w/pierced gilt-bronze scrolled crest & female terms at the corners above a curved & arched glazed cabinet door & rounded glazed sides all w/gilt-bronze trim, the conforming base w/gilt-bronze scrolls & a narrow inlaid panel; the conforming slightly stepped-out lower section w/serpentine edges above a pair of curved cupboard doors inlaid w/mother-of-pearl flowers & foliage within foliate-scrolled borders, the slender cabriole legs headed by foliate-cast female term mounts continuing down to leaf sabots & joined by a shaped stretcher shelf, France, ca. 1900, 34 1/4" w., 79" h. (ILLUS.) **$10,200**

Vitrine cabinet, Empire-Style, gilt-bronze mounted mahogany, the D-form red marble top w/a flat central section above a conforming frieze band mounted w/gilt-bronze griffins, sheaves of wheat & palmettes above a conforming case w/the wide flat glazed central door opening to glass shelves & flanked by gilt-bronze-mounted flat pilasters above a wide lower panel w/a large gilt-bronze mount of Apollo driving his chariot, the curved glass sides above lower panels w/gilt-bronze wreath mounts, molded apron on short peg feet, Antoine Krieger, Paris, early 20th c., 18 1/2 x 51", 72" h. **$9,000**

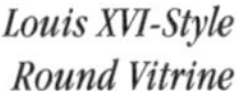

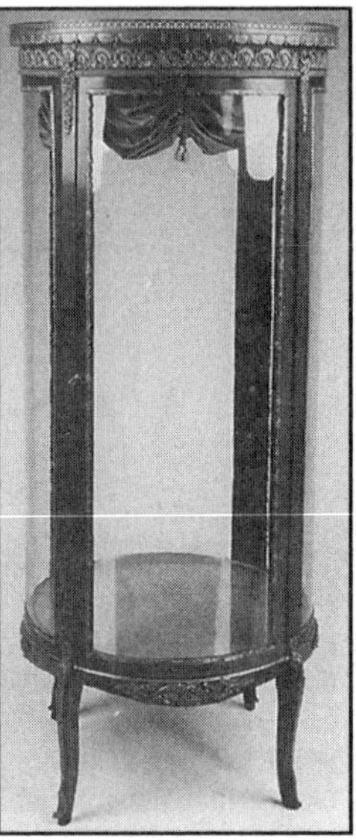

Louis XVI-Style Round Vitrine

Vitrine cabinet, Louis XV-Style, walnut, a rectangular red marble top atop the tall case w/a tall door w/a rectangular beveled glass front within a serpentine framework above a lower rectangular panel w/serpentine edges & ornate scroll carving, molded chamfered corner bands, scroll-carved serpentine apron & simple cabriole legs w/scroll carving & scroll & peg feet, France, late 19th - early 20th c., 15 1/2 x 32", 61" h. **$2,310**

Vitrine cabinet, Louis XVI-Style, gilt-metal mounted mahogany, round marble top w/a low pierced gilt-metal gallery above a conforming case w/four curved sides, two forming doors, doors w/thin gilt-metal banded trim w/further trim on the narrow rounded apron, raised on simple cabriole legs ending in sabots, France, late 19th to early 20th c., 25 3/4" d., 59" h. (ILLUS.) **$3,738**

One of Two Victorian Vitrine Cabinets

Vitrine cabinets, Victorian, ormolu-mounted inlaid satinwood, each w/oblong crossbanded molded top w/canted corners above glazed sides & a glazed door, the door w/an arched pane below a delicate inlaid leafy swag band, raised on a deep molded base w/bead-trimmed disk-topped peg feet, Europe, late 19th c., 10 x 28", 29 1/2" h., pr. (ILLUS. of one) **$5,98**

Chairs

Queen Anne Armchair

Chairs are a common form of furniture found in every design style and in every room setting. Simple ladderbacks were used as kitchen chairs, elegant suites of chairs graced the dining room, while easy chairs waited by the fire for their occupants.

Bedroom suites frequently included several matching side chairs and perhaps a rocker to match the bed and case pieces. A good chairmaker was an important member of early Colonial communities and found his work to be in demand. His craft was taught to apprentices and often they closely followed the examples at hand. Early design books were used as guides, but American ingenuity often adapted styles to suit available woods, etc.

During many of the early furniture styles, such as Chippendale, Federal, and Queen Anne, it was assumed that large pillows would be used on the seat, adding a little more comfort. Later styles, such as Arts & Crafts, featured cushions included as part of the

Fan Back Windsor

design and often made a statement by their use of leather or other coverings. As furniture became factory made, American furniture makers made many chairs to meet the ever-increasing demand for affordable furniture. Today, furniture buyers can choose from well-made craftsmen chairs that reflect early styles, mass-produced chairs readily available at furniture stores, and interesting designs by custom manufacturers.

It can be hard to determine whether a side chair began life as a dining room chair, bedroom chair, etc. One way to determine if chairs were originally sold as a set is to carefully examine the interior frame for signs of numbers. Often Roman numerals were used to indicate that it belonged to a set. These numerals were sometimes incised into the frame, while others were simple chalk markings.

Some terms that relate to chairs are:

Crest rail: the top rail on the back.

Side rail: side rails extending from the crest rail to seat.

Stretcher base: the structural members that extend from leg to leg, adding stability. An H-stretcher looks like its name implies. A box-stretcher is a bar from leg to leg. An X-stretcher goes across the base and the stretcher bars cross, sometimes joined together.

Splat: the decorative part of a back between the crest rail and seat. When shaped like a vase, it can be known as a "vasiform splat."

h seat: Seat height is often noted to help determine the original usage of a chair. This kind of information is important to consider to understand if a chair has been shortened because of damage, wear, removing casters, etc.

Back height: This "h" dimension indicates the height at the center of the back of the chair.

Over-upholstered: Upholstered section that appears to be overstuffed.

Adirondack-style Painted Armchair

Adirondack-style armchairs, composed of hickory sticks, the rectangular back frame enclosing seven spindles above the open round arms on curved supports continuing down to form front legs, woven splint seat, double front & side rungs, crackled white over earlier green paint, possibly New York state, early 20th c., 38 3/4" h., pr. (ILLUS. of one) **$805**

Art Deco Upholstered Armchair

Art Deco armchair, carved parcel-gilt mahogany & upholstery, the narrow gently arched gilt-trimmed crestrail above the upholstered back flanked by downswept closed upholstered arms w/carved hand rests atop tapering round front reeded legs, cushion seat, attributed to Sue et Mare, France, ca. 1925 (ILLUS.) **$4,600**

Art Deco armchairs, upholstered mahogany, a sloped upholstered backrest flanked by shaped plank arms centering a loose seat cushion raised on reeded round feet, attributed to Dominique, France, ca. 1925, pr. (upholstery distressed) **$6,325**

Art Deco Club chairs, walnut & leather-upholstered, the high lobed upholstered back continuing to the rounded arms centering a high tight seat raised on short feet on casters, upholstered in pale bluish grey leather upholstery, England, 1930s, pr. (wear at edges) **$1,380**

Art Nouveau Armchair

Art Nouveau armchair, fruitwood marquetry w/backsplat inlaid in various woods w/chestnuts & leafage, flanked by twist-carved spindles & molded arms above upholstered seat, raised on twist-carved front legs, Majorelle, France, ca. 1900 (ILLUS.) **$3,450**

Arts & Crafts armchair, oak, a wide gently curved crestrail above a back w/a pair of slender slats flanking a wide center slat w/two square cut-outs all resting on a lower back rail, flat open arms on flat front stile legs w/narrow tapering rectangular cut-outs, new black leather seat cushion, wide flat low stretchers, original finish, Limbert branded mark, 38 1/ 2" h. (small repair to rear leg) **$4,675**

Arts & Crafts chairs, oak, each w/a square-topped back stile flanking a shaped crestrail pierced w/a heart flanked by scrolls above three slender slats, shaped open arms, upholstered seat, squared tapering front legs, medium brown finish, England, early 20th c., two armchairs & four side chairs, 42 1/4" h., set of 6 (some wear) **$3,565**

Arts & Crafts Inlaid Rocking Chair

Arts & Crafts rocking chair w/arms, inlaid oak, a wide gently arched crestrail & flat lower rail flanking two plain slats & a shaped center splat w/Art Nouveau style looping foliate inlay, tapering stiles w/rounded tops, flat open arms on shaped armrests forming front legs, floral upholstered seat, flat stretchers, mortised rockers, medium brown finish, ca. 1910, 35" h. (ILLUS.) **$1,035**

Early Thonet Bentwood Side Chairs

Bentwood side chairs, a high tapering bentwood back frame enclosing a wide upper cross rail w/three holes above three slender spindles to a thin lower rail above the caned seat in a bentwood frame forming the front legs joined by a high flat stretcher, a forked downswept bentwood stretcher at each side of the base, Thonet, Austria, late 19th c., paint restoration, 38 1/2" h., pr. **$575**

Biedermeier-Style Side Chairs

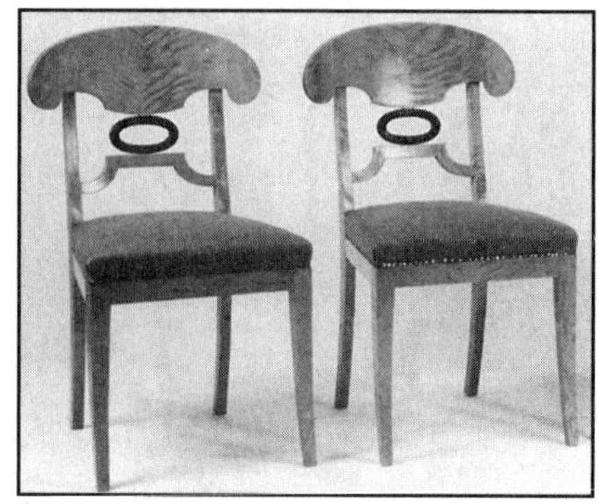

Biedermeier-Style side chairs, fruitwood & part-ebonized, wide arched & shaped crest above a small ebonized wreath on a shaped lower back rail flanked by simple stiles, overupholstered seat on gently curved square tapering legs, Europe, late 19th c., 32 1/2" h., set of four (ILLUS. of two) **$3,335**

Boston rocking chair w/arms, painted & decorated, the wide rounded crestrail above six tall spindles & simple turned stiles above the S-scroll arms on a spindle & turned canted arm support, deep S-scroll seat, knob- and rod-turned front legs w/a knob-turned front stretcher, plain turned side & back stretchers, worn original red & black graining w/yellow striping & stenciling w/fruit in colored bronze powder on the crest, early 19th c., 39 1/2" h. (rockers worn) **$220**

Fine Boston Chippendale Side Chair

Chippendale side chair, carved mahogany, the bow-shaped crestrail ending in scrolled terminals above a pierced & scroll-carved splat flanked by outward flaring stiles above a trapezoidal slip seat, front cabriole legs ending in pad feet on platforms, joined by turned stretchers to the raked chamfered rear legs, old finish, Boston or Salem, Massachusetts, ca. 1770, minor imperfections, 37 3/4" h. **$7,475**

Chippendale side chair, carved mahogany, the serpentine crestrail w/foliate-carved scrolled ears above a pierce-carved interlaced Gothic splat flanked by molded stiles over a trapezoidal seat & conforming slipseat on cabriole front legs ending in ball-and-claw feet, Philadelphia, ca. 1770, 38 1/4" h. **$8,625**

Chippendale side chair, carved mahogany, the shaped leaf- and volute-carved crestrail above a pierced strapwork splat & overupholstered seat on acanthus-carved cabriole legs joined by

Chippendale Wing Chair

block- and baluster-turned stretchers & ending in claw-and-ball feet, old surface w/dark brown color, Boston, Massachusetts, ca. 1770, 37" h. **$4,600**

Chippendale wing armchair, walnut, the arched upholstered back flanked by slightly flared serpentined upholstered wings above rolled upholstered arms above the wide cushion seat, square molded legs joined by box stretchers, late 18th c. (ILLUS.) **$3,850**

Chippendale-Style dining chairs, walnut, a serpentine crestrail centering a carved shell flanked by scrolled ears above a pierced vasiform splat over a trapezoidal slip seat above a shaped seatrail centering a carved shell, on cabriole legs w/ball-and-claw feet, two armchairs w/downscrolling arms w/hand holds over shaped arm supports, four side chairs, in the Philadelphia manner, 20th c., the set **$4,025**

Large Classical Revival Armchair

Classical Revival armchair, carved oak, the wide square upholstered back flanked by large boldly carved seated winged lions forming the arms, a wide spring-upholstered seat above a leaf-carved seat frame raised on canted front legs ending in large paw feet, square tapering rear legs, leather upholstery, refinished, American-made, ca. 1880-90, 40" h. (ILLUS.) **$5,500**

Fine Boston Classical Side Chairs

Classical side chairs, mahogany & mahogany veneer, the concave veneered crestrails w/leaf-carved terminals atop shaped stiles joined by scroll-carved slats above the upholstered slip seats & molded seatrail, incurved front legs & outswept rear legs, old refinish, very minor imperfections, Boston, 1825-35, set of 4 (ILLUS. of two) **$2,300**

Country-style armchairs, stained maple, the squared back panel of tightly woven splint between projecting backswept stiles w/long shaped open arms on baluster-turned arm supports continuing down to form side braces, tightly woven splint seat, sim-

Woven Splint Armchairs

ple turned legs w/plain turned double front & side & rear stretchers, splints partially distressed, minor chips to feet, back of stiles worn, late 19th - early 20th c., 34 1/2" h., pr. (ILLUS.) **$805**

Country-style arrow-back side chairs, decorated, wide crestrail above four curved arrow slats between the curved tapering stiles, shaped saddle seat on bamboo-turned legs joined by a turned front stretcher & plain turned side stretchers, original red decoration, the crestrail w/yellow & green foliage, usual stretcher wear, early 19th c., 35" h., set of 4 .... **$2,970**

Country-style banister-back side chair, carved maple, the tall back w/baluster- and knob-turned stiles & ball finials above a fan-carved crestrail above four split-balusters continuing to a lower rail w/an arched pendant, the woven splint seat on baluster-, ring- and rod- turned legs joined by two swelled front

Early Ladder-Back Armchair

stretchers & simple turned side & back stretchers, traces of dark green stain, probably New Hampshire, second half 18th c., 44 1/2" h. (reduced in height) **$4,600**

Country-style ladder-back armchair, maple & ash, four arched slats joining knob- and rod-turned stiles w/knob finials over long scrolled arms on baluster- and knob-turned arm supports continuing into turned front legs, woven splint seat, double knob-turned front stretchers & plain double side stretchers, old painted surface, restored, probably Massachusetts, early 18th c., 45 1/2" h. (ILLUS.) **$546**

Danish Modern dining chairs, teak, each w/a swelled arched crestrail curving to form a U-form rail w/slender flattened open arms all supported on four slightly canted turned & swelled supports flanking the caned seat, designed by Hans Wegner, each branded Johannes Hansen Copenhagen Denmark, ca. 1949, set of 12 .... **$28,750**

Early Ladder-Back Armchair

Danish Modern rocking chair w/arms, teak, a curved crestrail & arms on tapering squared stile legs joined by slender arched seatrails, on rockers, woven rust-colored back & seat cushions, foil label of M. Nissan, Denmark, 28" h. **$173**

Early American country-style ladder-back armchair, probably maple, the tall back w/five arched slats between turned stiles w/oblong finials, the shaped open arms w/baluster-turned arm supports continuing to the front legs & flanking the replaced woven rush seat, double knob- and baluster-turned stretchers in the front & simple turned stretchers at the sides & back, original dark finish, ca. 1820, 46" h. (ILLUS.) **$350**

Federal Leather & Wood Armchair

Federal armchair, mahogany, butternut & leather, the ring-turned slender crestrail above the raking leather-upholstered back, downward scrolling open arms on urn-shaped arm supports on a wide leather-upholstered seat over ring- and baluster-turned tapering front legs on peg feet, square back stile legs, original surface & leather, minor imperfections, possibly Portsmouth, New Hampshire, early 19th c., 40" h. **$1,150**

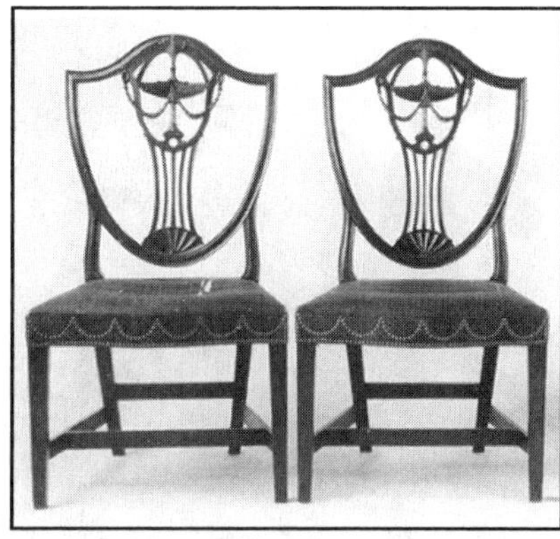

Part of Federal Shield-back Chair Set

Federal side chairs, carved mahogany, shield-back style, the arched & molded crestrail & molded stiles above a carved kylix splat w/festoons draped from flanking carved rosettes, above a pierced splat terminating in a carved lunette at its base above the molded rear seatrail & overupholstered seat w/serpentine front, square tapering front & canted rear legs joined by flat stretchers, seats w/old black horsehair, old surface, Rhode Island or Salem, Massachusetts, ca. 1795, four side chairs & matching armchair, armchair w/arm restoration, 37 3/4" h., the set (ILLUS. of two) **$23,000**

Louis XV Revival Upholstered Armchair

Louis XV Revival armchair, mahogany, the oval medallion back w/figural needlepoint upholstery w/brass tack trim, arched & shaped padded open arms on carved incurved arms over the wide needlepoint-upholstered spring seat w/brass tack trim, serpentine seatrail w/shell and scroll carving, carved cabriole front legs ending in scroll feet on pegs, original finish, ca. 1920s, 38" h. **$650**

Gustav Stickley Armchair

Mission-style (Arts & Crafts movement) armchair, oak, a top & lower back rail flanking three wide slats between the slender square back stiles over flat shaped arms on square front leg stiles w/corbels under the arms, replaced upholstered seat, recent finish, unsigned Gustav Stickley, Model No. 340, 41" h. **$605**

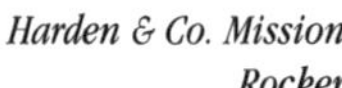
Harden & Co. Mission Rocker

Mission-style (Arts & Crafts movement) rocking chair w/arms, oak, a wide curved crestrail over four narrow & one wide vertical slats flanked by square stiles, flat shaped open arms on front leg supports w/side corbels, spring cushion leather seat, paper label of Harden and Co., early 20th c., some stains & roughness, 37" h. **$518**

Eames "DCW" Side Chairs

Modern style "DCW" side chairs, walnut plywood, wide curved back panel on curved support over the dished wide curved seat, arched tapering canted legs, designed by Charles Eames, w/paper label, ca. 1950s, 28" h., pr. (ILLUS.) **$546**

Pilgrim Century "Carver" armchair, turned maple, the baluster- and rod-turned stiles topped w/ball finials w/two turned rails centering three turned spindles, the turned front posts w/ball finials above the rush seat, plain turned box stretchers, old dry finish, dark brown color, Rhode Island, 1670-1700, 39 1/2" h. (feet worn, chips throughout, right arm & right stretcher probably replaced) **$7,475**

Pilgrim Century "Great Chair," turned & joined oak, the flame & ring finials above turned & incised stiles centering a double-baluster & ring-turned crest over three tapering spindles, all above cylindrical open arms & bun-turned hand grips over turned front post legs over a trapezoidal rush seat, on cylindrical legs joined by double box stretchers, Plymouth County, Massachusetts, 1715-30, 38 3/4" h. **$8,050**

New England Queen Anne Armchair

Queen Anne armchair, maple, the yoked crestrail over a vasiform splat & molded stay-rail flanked by raked stiles joining scrolling molded arms on baluster-, block- and ring-turned supports continuing to front legs, joined by a bulbous turned front stretcher & square side & back stretchers to the raked rear legs, vestiges of old red stain, New England, ca. 1740-60, minor imperfections, 40 3/4" h. **$9,200**

Country Queen Anne Painted Chair

Queen Anne country-style side chair, carved & painted, the arched & carved crestrail above a tall vasiform splat & molded raked stiles, the rush seat on block-, baluster- and ring-turned front legs joined by bulbous turned front & side stretchers, retains old burnt sienna & dark brown paint w/yellow pinstriping, New England, 18th c., 41" h. **$1,495**

Victorian Aesthetic Movement Armchair

Victorian Aesthetic Movement corner armchairs, ebonized & parcel-gilt, flat crestrails forming square corner w/each back section centered by a panel of gilt stenciled stylized birds & geometric designs flanked by short ring-turned spindles all raised above the over-upholstered seat on a line-incised gilt-trimmed seatrail on chamfered legs ending in casters, Kimbel and Cabus, New York, New York, ca. 1870s, 27 1/2" h., pr. (ILLUS. of one) **$4,485**

Baroque Revival Armchair

Victorian Baroque Revival armchair, carved mahogany, a flat pierce-carved crestrail flanked by squared, pointed finials above the wide upholstered back, scrolled open arms ending in carved faces above the carved square tapering armrests above the wide upholstered seat, ring-, ball- and block-turned legs on low blocked feet, legs joined by a turned H-stretcher, original finish, late 19th c., 42" h. **$650**

Unique Classical Revival Armchair

Victorian Classical Revival armchair, oak & walnut, the tall back w/a fan-carved rounded crestrail above a pierce-carved back w/a lyre-form splat carved w/bold scrolls, the back stiles w/square knob finials above narrow shaped side wings above the wide flat arms w/ scrolled hand grips raised on a flat armrest, the long caned trapezoidal seat lifting to expose a hole for a chamber pot, deep apron, simple turned front legs on casters, origi-nal finish, last quarter 19th c., 40" h. **$250**

Victorian Balloon-back Side Chairs

Victorian country-style ballon-back side chairs, painted & decorated, a rounded back rail w/tapering stiles centered by a vase-form splat, shaped plank seat on ring- and rod- turned front legs joined by a turned stretcher, plain turned rear legs & plain turned side & rear stretchers, the crestrail decorated w/a stenciled basket of fruit above the splat stenciled w/an eagle & shield w/Union, gilt vine stenciled border, stiles, seat & legs w/yellow & salmon striping, Pennsylvania, ca. 1860, some paint wear, 33 1/2" h., pr. **$460**

Ornate Golden Oak Rocking Chiar

Victorian Golden Oak rocking chair w/arms, quarter-sawn oak, the tall back w/two scalloped crestrails joined by a central roundel & a row of tiny spindles, the upper rail w/stylized lion-carved ears, over a slender center carved vase-form splat flanked by slender bead-turned spindles all flanked by knob- and rod-turned stiles, shaped flat arms over knob-turned spindles & arm rests above a shaped round pressed composition seat (not shown), ring- and knob-turned front legs joined by double turned stretchers, refinished, ca. 1890s, 45" h. **$350**

Victorian Gothic Revival Side Chairs

Victorian Gothic Revival side chairs, mahogany & mahogany veneer, rounded & peaked molded crestrail over a veneered panel above four slender ring- and baluster-turned spindles forming five Gothic arches, the lower rail raised above the upholstered slip seat, simple flattened cabriole front legs & canted rear legs, ca. 1850, 32" h., set of 10 (ILLUS. of two) **$1,380**

Victorian Neo-Grec Armchair

Victorian Neo-Grec armchairs, ebonized & gilt-trimmed hardwood, the canted & back-scrolled crest w/upholstered central panel above a frame enclosing seven short turned spindles flanked by conforming gilt-incised stiles leading to downscrolling upholstered arms & arched, gilt-incised armrests over similarly incised downscrolling side rails flanking the rectangular upholstered seat, on a carved & gilt-incised curule-form base joined by a turned stretcher, on casters, American, ca. 1870, 34 1/4" h., pr. (ILLUS. of one) **$3,680**

Victorian Renaissance Revival Chair

Victorian Renaissance Revival side chairs, carved rosewood, the tall upholstered back w/a high scroll- and architectural-carved crestrail centered by a carved maidenhead above incurved stiles over the serpentine upholstered seat on a conforming seatrail w/central carved drop, on boldly turned & tapering trumpet legs on casters, red silk upholstery, attributed to John Jelliff, ca. 1870, 38 1/2" h., pr. (ILLUS. of one) .. **$978**

Rococo Carved Rosewood Armchair

Victorian Rococo armchair, carved rosewood, the tall upholstered balloon back w/a high arched & pierce-carved crest w/bold fruit & floral carving on the molded frame raised above the upholstered spring seat flanked by padded shaped open arms w/incurved supports, serpentine seatrail w/nut-carved center, on demi-cabriole front legs on original casters, refinished, new upholstery, ca. 1860, 44" h. **$1,200**

Meeks-style Rosewood Slipper Chair

Victorian Rococo slipper chair, carved & laminated rosewood, the tall balloon-form wood back ornately pierce-carved w/tight scrolls & grape clusters below a high arched & rope twist-carved crest, the deep upholstered spring seat on a narrow seatrail w/a carved front medallion between the short carved & shaped front legs, attributed to J. & J.W. Meeks, New York City, ca. 1855, old reupholstery, original finish, ca. 1855, 42" h. **$1,600**

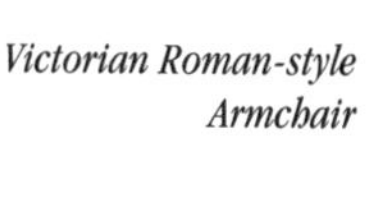

Victorian Roman-style Armchair

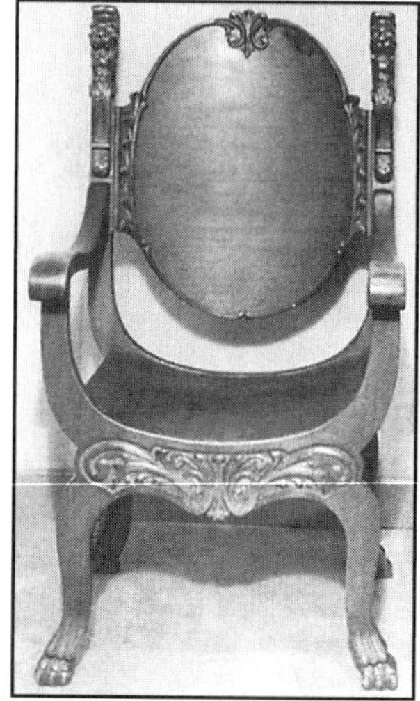

Victorian Roman-style chairs, mahogany & mahogany veneer, armchair & matching rocker, each w/a large oval back panel w/delicate scroll-carved borders suspended between heavy carved stiles topped by carved lions head w/"jeweled" eyes, heavy shaped open arms on U-form supports enclosing the solid curved seat, wide scroll-carved seatrail continuing to flattened cabriole legs ending in large paw feet, old dark finish, one arm support w/glued break, ca. 1900, armchair 42" h., pr. (ILLUS. of armchair) **$550**

Windsor Arrow-back Highchair

Windsor arrow-back highchair, painted, a stepped crestrail raised on backswept tapering stiles flanking three long curved arrow slats over simple turned arms on bamboo-turned spindles over the thick shaped plank seat, tall canted swelled bamboo-turned legs w/a front footrest over a high turned swelled stretcher & matching rear stretcher, lower side stretchers, early red paint, very minor surface imperfections, New England, 1820-30, 36" h. **$2,875**

Painted Birdcage Windsor Side Chair

Windsor birdcage side chairs, painted, the birdcage crestrail w/three short over seven long spindles flanked by turned stiles on a shaped, incised saddle seat, four splayed bamboo-turned legs joined by matching stretchers, overall old red paint w/yellow accents & yellow seat, the stiles w/leaf decoration, New England, ca. 1810, seats repainted, 34 1/ 4" h., pr. (ILLUS. of one) **$1,850**

Painted Windsor Comb-back Rocker

Windsor comb-back rocking chair w/arms, painted & decorated pine & maple, the tall comb w/a rectangular crestrail over five slender spindles above the shaped back crestrail flanked by rabbit-ear curved stiles flanking five tall slender spindles, S-scroll arms on a spindle & canted arm support over the wide dished plank seat, simple turned canted legs on inset rockers, original painted & stenciled decoration w/blossoms & leaves on the crestrails against a dark brown ground, ca. 1830, 46" h. **$450**

Painted Continuous Arm Windsor

Windsor continuous-arm armchair, painted, the arched crestrail continuing to flat arms & hand holds above seven spindles & baluster- and ring-turned canted arm supports, shaped saddle seat on bamboo-turned canted legs joined by a swelled H-stretcher, old salmon red paint, attributed to Ebenezer Tracy, Jr., New London County, Connecticut, ca. 1800, 35 1/2" h. **$3,105**

Windsor continuous-arm armchairs, each w/a molded bowed back continuing down to slender shaped arms, seven slender bamboo-turned back spindles & two short spindles under each arm w/a canted baluster- and ring-turned arm support, wide shaped saddle seat on canted bamboo-turned legs joined by a swelled H-stretcher, old brown finish, size varies so possibly a ladys & gentlemans set, attributed to Connecticut, possibly by Beriah Green, Windham County, 37" & 39 3/4" h., pr. **$5,225**

Windsor continuous-arm brace-back armchair, painted, the slender arched crestrail curving down to form slender arms w/scrolled grips above numerous slender turned spindles & canted baluster- and ring-turned arm supports, shaped saddle seat, on canted baluster-, ring- and rod-turned tapering legs joined by a swelled H-stretcher, old black paint, New York, school of W. MacBride, 18th c. **$2,500**

Windsor "fan-back" armchair, ash & maple, the shaped crestrail above eight tall spindles & a U-form central rail continuing to form shaped arms on baluster- and ring-turned arm supports & six additional short spindles, wide shaped saddle seat, splayed baluster- and ring-turned legs joined by a swelled H-stretcher, refinished, New England, ca. 1790, 46" h. **$3,738**

Windsor "fan-back" rocking armchair, serpentine crestrail w/downscrolling ear volutes above ring- and baluster-turned & blocked stiles centered by nine tapering spindles over shaped arms terminating in downscrolling knuckled hand holds above ring- and baluster-turned arm supports over a shaped plank seat, on ring- and baluster-turned legs joined by a baluster-turned H-stretcher, shaped rockers, early 19th c., 39" h. **$1,610**

Fine Windsor Fan-back Armchair

Windsor fan-back armchair, painted, a long serpentine crestrail w/scroll-carved terminals above nine tall spindles, a medial armrail ending in scrolled carved hand holds on baluster- and ring-turned arm supports, shaped saddle seat, canted baluster-, ring- and rod- turned legs joined by a swelled H-stretcher, New England, ca. 1780, 43 1/2" h. **$5,463**

Windsor fan-back side chair, painted, the serpentine crestrail over nine spindles flanked by ring- and baluster-turned canted stiles over the shaped saddle seat on canted baluster- and ring-turned legs joined by a swelled H-stretcher, old green paint, Connecticut, 1790-1810, 40" h. (paint wear & loss) **$3,450**

Windsor fan-back writing-arm armchair, painted, a small shaped crestrail above five tall slender spindles above the U-form mid-rail continuing at one side to form a wide writing surface w/two small drawers beneath, numerous slender swelled spindles from mid-rail to wide shaped seat over a small drawer, raised on canted bamboo-turned legs joined by a bamboo-turned H-stretcher, old black paint, New England, early 19th c., 42 1/2" h. (restoration to drawers) **$4,025**

Windsor low-back writing-arm armchair, country-style, a curved shaped crestrail continuing to form arms ending in knuckled armrests & a wide teardrop-shaped writing surface at one side above a small bowed drawer all raised on simple bamboo-turned spindles, a wide shaped plank seat on canted bamboo-turned legs joined by turned box stretchers, overall worn black paint, Vermont, late 18th - early 19th c. **$5,200**

Windsor "rabbit-ear" side chairs, painted & decorated, a wide gently curved top crestrail over two thin lower rails over four short turned spindles above the seat all between backswept tapering rabbit-ear stiles, rounded thick plank seat on canted bamboo-turned legs joined by box stretchers, yellow painted ground w/stenciled fruit & leaf designs in green & raw umber w/gilt highlights on the crestrail, dark striping, old repaint, New England, ca. 1830-40, 33 1/2" h., set of 6 (imperfections) **$3,220**

Early Sack-back Windsor Armchair

Windsor sack-back armchair, painted, the bowed crestrail over seven spindles continuing through the medial rail that extends to form narrow shaped arms over spindle & baluster- and ring-turned canted arm supports, wide oblong saddle seat, on slightly splayed ring- and baluster-turned tapering legs joined by a swelled H-stretcher, old green paint over earlier black, imperfections, southeastern New England, ca. 1780, 38 1/2" h. **$3,335**

Chests

Chippendale Highboy

Chests of drawers are a furniture form found in all design styles. Sizes, woods, and ornamentation vary from style to style.

The phrase "overlapping drawer" refers to a slight extension on the face of the drawer that covers the drawer opening tightly when closed, thus overlapping the case. The phrase "graduated" means the drawers are different in size from one to another; usually the smallest drawer is on the top, the next one slightly larger, etc. Both "cockbeaded" and "thumbmolded" refer to different types of molding that were used as decoration. The terms "bow front" and "serpentine" describe the shape of the front of a chest of drawers. A "bow front" is generally slightly swelled, or bowed, in the center. "Serpentine" describes a more shaped top, often having several curves. Both bow front and serpentine chests of drawers will have a flat back.

Because chests of drawers were popular pieces of furniture, many homes had more than one, resulting in many examples available to the antiques marketplace. Some of these beautiful chests of drawers were made by early local craftsmen, and a few are signed or easily identified with a maker or geographic region. As furniture became mass-produced, chests of drawers kept their appeal and the form remained popular.

Chests of drawers offered a cabinetmaker an opportunity to use fine woods and elegant brass hardware. When a description includes the phrase "secondary wood," that refers to the wood used on the interior of the drawers, perhaps the back, or areas that are unseen. This practice allowed the cabinetmaker to keep his costs down by using only expensive wood for the exterior case. It is also theorized that this practice allowed the cabinetmaker to use lesser-quality native wood that he had readily available, saving the expensive mahogany for the front and top. Today, by studying the secondary wood, dealers and auctioneers gain an important clue as to the region of origin and sometimes the time frame.

Some other names for chests of drawers are dressers, chests, or bureaus, usually depending on the geographic nature of language rather than a difference in style.

Several forms of chests of drawers are found in the antique marketplace. Among these are highboys, lowboys, chests on chests, and tall chests.

Empire Mule Chest

Many of these chests were made in two or more pieces. This was done to facilitate moving the large pieces, and it was probably easier for the craftsman, too. While it is quite normal to see highboys and other large chests in museums and restored historic properties, it is important to remember that these were often originally made for storage and intended to be used in bedrooms as well as other rooms. Because architecture has changed as much as furniture styles, consideration had to be given to how these big pieces would get up stairs, etc. Look for signs of carrying handles on many of the large two-piece chests.

The ability to "show off" one's important furniture was important to our Colonial ancestors. These massive pieces of furniture were clear signs of one's wealth and stature in the community. The best hardware was used, and careful attention was paid to the maintenance of these large case pieces, too. With the current trend for original finishes in today's antiques marketplace, what we often fail to remember is that many times these pieces were made of lesser woods than the fine mahogany used so often in smaller chests of drawers. Elaborate finishes were created trying to duplicate the graining of mahogany and other expensive woods. Many of these original finishes have been removed over the years. How much the original finish adds to the provenance and value of the piece is very much determined by a potential buyer.

Some of the early craftsmen who created these masterpieces did sign their work. Look closely at the backboards or in drawers or even under drawers for such a signature. Finding a documented craftsman's name will add greatly to the value. As in other types of furniture, styles and woods used varied from one geographic region to another. By carefully studying these changes, auctioneers, collectors, appraisers, antiques dealers, and curators are able to discern where a particular piece originated.

See also Highboys & Lowboys.

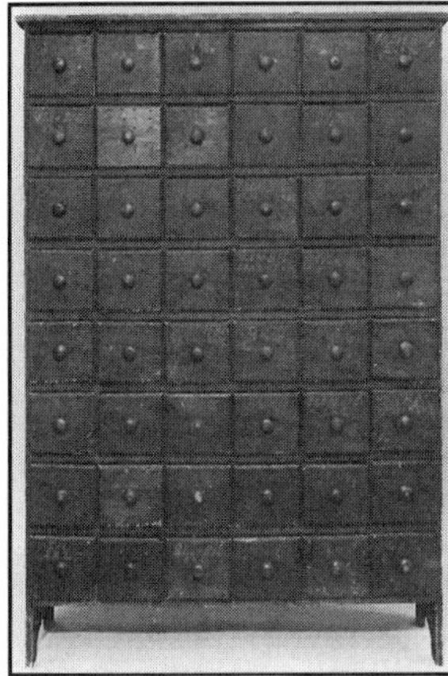

Early Apothecary-style Chest

Apothecary chest, stained wood, rectangular top slightly overhanging tall case of 48 square drawers w/turned wood pulls & beveled edges, sizes & lettering on most drawers, wire nail construction, bootjack ends, old black stain, probably used by a cobbler or saddle maker, 19th c., minor edge chips, 13 x 42 1/2", 62" h. (ILLUS.) **$4,070**

Apothecary chest, painted & decorated pine, a rectangular top on the dovetailed case enclosing 64 small square numbered drawers w/small knobs above a row of three deep drawers across the bottom, grain-painted overall in light brown on tan to resemble mahogany, probably New England, early 19th c., 14 1/4 x 43", 39" h. (imperfections) **$10,925**

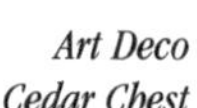

Art Deco Cedar Chest

Apothecary chest, painted pine, a rectangular top above a short open compartment across the top of the tall case containing rows of 20 large drawers over a lower section of 16 graduated small drawers, various wood & brass knobs & remnants of labels, square nail construction, old worn brown & tan grained repaint, 19th c., 15 1/2 x 48 1/4", 66" h. **$3,520**

Art Deco cedar chest, red cedar-lined w/mixed rosed & mahogany exterior veneering, a low stepped crestrail centered by a built-in electric clock & w/small hanky drawers over the rectangular top lifting above a deep well, the front w/elaborate light & dark veneering w/incised angular line detail above a pair of long bottom drawers w/yellow Bakelite pulls, on square legs on a trestle base, refinished, ca. 1930s, 20 x 44", 30" h. (ILLUS.) **$400**

Chippendale Child's Blanket Chest

Blanket chest, child's, Chippendale country-style, painted pine, six-board construction, a hinged rectangular top w/molded edges above a dovetailed case on a molded base w/scroll-cut bracket feet, original mustard yellow & brown grain paint to resemble exotic wood, probably New England, late 18th c., repairs, 12 x 20 1/2", 14" h. (ILLUS.) **$1,850**

Blanket chest, country-style, painted & decorated poplar, a rectangular hinged top w/molded edges opening to a deep well, dovetailed case w/applied moldings & a pair of narrow bottom drawers above the narrow curved apron & bracket feet, original red paint w/black & yellow trim & gold-stenciled decoration including foliage, flowers & "Jeremias Wever, 1859, Mf. by C.C.B.," drawer divider a cut-out small panel w/heart & circles in black over yellow, old round glass drawer pulls, replaced inlaid escutcheons, Soap Hollow, Pennsylvania, 22 3/4 x 49 1/2", 28 1/2" h. (minor repairs to feet, some edge damage & wear) **$11,000**

Blanket chest, painted & decorated poplar, Sonnenberg-type, rectangular hinged top w/molded edges opening to a well w/a lidded till, dovetailed base w/bottom flat molding, simple bracket feet, decorated w/original dark red paint ground w/yellow stripe-edged reserves w/polychrome floral designs on the front panel, yellow striping & a compass star in red & yellow on the top, 19th c., 19 3/8 x 37 5/8", 23 1/4" h. **$10,450**

Blanket chest, Chippendale country-style, walnut, a rectangular hinged lid w/molded edges opening to a well w/till, dovetailed case w/original brass butterfly keyhole escutcheon, a mid-molding above a lower row of three drawers each w/butterfly pulls above the molded base on ogee bracket feet, wrought-iron bear-trap lock, mellow finish, Pennsylvania, attributed to Chester County, late 18th - early 19th c., 24 1/4 x 55", 29" h. (slight warp in lid) **$4,950**

Chippendale chest of drawers, cherry, a rectangular top w/molded edges & serpentine front above a conforming case w/four long graduated cockbeaded drawers w/butterfly pulls & keyhole escutcheons, molded base on scroll-cut ogee bracket feet, Hartford, Connecticut, ca. 1770-80, 22 1/2 x 34", 32 1/2" h. (ILLUS.) **$17,250**

Fine Chippendale Chest of Drawers

Chippendale chest-on-chest, maple, two-part construction: the upper section w/a rectangular top & deep cove molding above a case of five long graduated drawers w/simple bail pulls; lower section w/a mid-molding above a slightly stepped-out case of four long graduated drawers w/simple bail pulls, brass oval keyhole escutcheons, base molding above the apron w/a carved central drop & scroll-carved bracket feet, old pulls, refinished, possibly Massachusetts or New Hampshire, ca. 1760-80, 18 1/2 x 36", 76" h. (minor repairs) **$14,950**

Chippendale tall chest of drawers, cherry & maple, a rectangular top above a deep coved cornice over a case w/a top central deep fan-carved drawer flanked by a stack of two small drawers on each side above six long graduated drawers, molded base on

Classical Mahogany Butler's Chest

tall scroll-cut bracket feet, oval brass pulls appear to be original, old finish, probably Connecticut, 18th c., added casters, 18 x 37", 62 3/4" h. (minor restoration) **$46,000**

Classical butlers chest, mahogany & mahogany veneer, a rectangular black marble top w/rounded front corners above an ogee-fronted false drawer folding down to form a writing surface & enclosing a fitted interior above three long working drawers w/original panel-cut glass pulls, deep molded base on corner block feet, French polish finish, ca. 1840, 18 x 42", 38" h. (ILLUS.) **$1,800**

Classical Mahogany Chest of Drawers

Classical chest of drawers, carved mahogany & mahogany veneer, a flat-topped scroll-ended top backboard above a row of three short drawers stepped back on the rectangular top over a pair of overhanging deep drawers above three long drawers flanked by columns w/a carved pineapple over leaf bands & a spiral-carved section, molded conforming base on heavy knob-, ring- and baluster-turned tapering legs, replaced early glass pulls, refinished, imperfections, North Shore Massachusetts, ca. 1825, 22 x 42 3/ 4", 45" h. **$978**

Curly Maple Classical Tall Chest

Classical country-style tall chest of drawers, curly maple, a rectangular top over a pair of drawers over four long graduated drawers flanked by baluster- and ring-turned free- standing columns, molded base on heavy turned ovoid front feet on casters, first half 19th c. **$715**

Early Pennsylvania Dower Chest

Dower chest, painted & decorated, a rectangular top w/molded edges opening to a well, the front decorated w/a large arch-topped rectangular panel centered by a large spread-winged eagle w/shield & banner in its beak, pinwheels, compass stars & tulips around the bird, in dark shades of umber, black, red & yellow within a red & white border, the background w/a finely sponged black & brown ground, black base molding & scroll-cut bracket feet, light surface cleaning, several spurs replaced, Center County, Pennsylvania, ca. 1814 .... **$12,500**

Federal Mahogany Chest-on-Chest

Federal chest-on-chest, inlaid mahogany & mahogany veneer, two-part construction: the upper section w/a rectangular top & widely flaring stepped cornice over a wide line-inlaid frieze band above a pair of drawers over three long graduated drawers w/inlaid ivory diamond keyhole escutcheons & simple turned wood pulls; the lower section w/a mid-molding over a case w/three long graduated drawers matching upper drawers, curved apron & high simple bracket feet, old finish w/original painted side decoration, section of side molding missing, several veneer chips & puttied repairs, late 18th - early 19th c., 24 x 44", 80" h. **$3,740**

Federal Birch & Cherry Chest

Federal country-style chest of drawers, wavy birch & grained cherry, the double-arched & scroll-cut top splashboard above a rectangular top w/ovolo front corners over ring-turned colonettes flanking four long graduated drawers w/oval brass pulls, raised on ring- and baluster-turned legs w/knob feet, old refinish, North Shore, Massachusetts, early 19th c., replaced brasses, imperfections, 17 1/2 x 39 1/2", 49" h. **$1,380**

Federal Cherry Sugar Chest

Federal country-style sugar chest, cherry, a rectangular hinged top w/molded edges opening to a deep divided interior well above a pair of small drawers, baluster- and ring-turned legs w/peg feet, paneled sides, oval drawer brasses, early 19th c., 16 1/2 x 35 1/ 2", 35" h. **$6,050**

Fine Inlaid Federal Tall Chest

Federal tall chest of drawers, inlaid walnut, rectangular top w/a wide coved cornice above a narrow diamond-inlaid frieze band above a row of three small drawers over five long graduated drawers all w/line-inlaid oval bands, oval brasses & diamond-form inlaid keyhole escutcheons, narrow inlaid banding down front stiles, veneered band around the base, on tall French feet, soft rubbed-out finish, Pennsylvania, late 18th - early 19th c., 24 3/4 x 46", 66 1/2" h. **$6,325**

French Provincial-Style Tall Chest

French Provincial-Style tall chest of drawers, inlaid walnut, a rectangular top w/serpentine ends above a tall case w/six long graduated drawers w/oblong panels centered by light wood leafy scroll inlays, paneled sides, serpentine apron, simple cabriole legs ending in scroll feet, keys used to pull open each drawer, original finish, ca. 1920s, 18 x 36", 5' h. **$600**

George III-Style Chest of Drawers

George III-Style bow-front chest of drawers, inlaid satinwood, rectangular top w/bowed front over a case w/four long graduated bowed drawers w/inlaid banding over the serpentine apron continuing to tall French feet, oval brass & metal keyhole escutcheons, small veneer losses, England, ca. 1900, 20 1/2 x 33", 33" h. **$4,600**

Georgian-Style Chest on Chest

Georgian-Style chest on chest, mahogany & mahogany veneer, two-part construction: the upper section w/a rectangular top w/cut front corners over a narrow cornice above three long deep drawers flanked by chamfered reeded edges; the lower section w/a mid-molding over two long, deep drawers, all w/butterfly brasses & keyhole escutcheons, molded base & serpentine apron on simple bracket feet, England, late 19th - early 20th c. **$800**

Rare G. Stickley Chest of Drawers

Mission-style (Arts & Crafts movement) chest of drawers, oak, a low crestrail above the rectangular top above a case w/a pair of short drawers over four long drawers, vertical pull plates on drawers form two bands up the front, paneled end w/cut-out feet, branded mark of Gustav Stickley, Model No. 906, ca. 1912, 21 x 41", 48" h. (ILLUS.) **$13,800**

Fine Gustav Stickley Tall Chest

Mission-style (Arts & Crafts movement) tall chest of drawers, oak, a low crest-board above the tall case w/slightly bowed side stiles & three pairs of small drawers over three long graduated drawers all w/turned wood knobs, arched apron, designed by Harvey Ellis, red decal mark of Gustav Stickley, Model No. 913, lightly cleaned original finish, slight veneer split, 20 x 36", 51" h. **$7,700**

Heywood-Wakefield Vanity Chest

Modern style vanity chest, maple, a large, tall upright rectangular back mirror w/rounded corners at one end above a glass shelf & open compartment, a case w/three graduated drawers at the other end, each w/tapering applied finger grip pulls, short block feet, wheat colored finish, round branded mark of Heywood-Wakefield, ca. 1950s, light wear, 13 1/4 x 53 3/4", base 24" h. (ILLUS.) **$345**

Mule chest (box chest w/one or more drawers below a storage compartment), Classical country-style, painted & decorated pine, a rectangular hinged top w/molded edges opening to a deep well faced w/two false drawers above two matching working drawers all w/turned wood knobs, on bulbous baluster- and ring-turned legs, original reddish brown graining in imitation of flame figured wood w/line inlay, black feet, found in New Hampshire, first half 19th c., 18 3/4 x 40", 40" h. (minor edge damage) **$1,650**

Early Painted Mule Chest

Mule chest (box chest w/one or more drawers below a storage compartment), painted pine, a rectangular hinged top opening to a deep well w/two false drawers at the front above two working drawers, all w/simple butterfly pulls & keyhole escutcheons, molded base on bootjack end legs, repainted greyish brown, probably Massachusetts, early 18th c., replaced brasses, 18 x 39 1/2", 37" h. (ILLUS.) **$1,150**

Mule chest (box chest w/one or more drawers below a storage compartment), Federal country-style, painted pine, a hinged rectangular top w/molded edges opening to a well w/two false long drawer fronts w/oval brasses above two long matching working drawers, original greyish blue vinegar graining on a greyish olive ground w/black & yellow edge striping, shaped apron on high tapering feet, bottom signed Daniel, attributed to Essex, Massachusetts, early 19th c., 19 3/8 x 42 3/4", 41 3/4" h. **$7,700**

Early Pilgrim Century Joined Chest

Pilgrim Century blanket chest, oak & pine, joined construction, the overhanging thumb-molded hinged white pine top above a three-paneled front w/applied moldings over a long drawer flanked by shadow molded stiles, recessed panel sides, the drawer w/stippled inscription "1707 HI," interior open till, old dark stained surface, New Haven Colony, Connecticut, 1680-1740, minor imperfections, 19 1/4 x 43", 31 1/2" h. (ILLUS.) **$9,775**

Queen Anne chest-on-frame, maple, two-part construction: the upper section w/a rectangular top w/a deep stepped cornice above a case of four long graduated thumb-molded drawers w/butterfly brasses & keyhole escutcheons; the lower section w/a mid-molding above a single long narrow drawer over the apron w/two drop pendants flanking a small central carved fan, cabriole legs ending in high pad feet, old refinished surface, Newburyport, 1750-80, 15 1/2 x 36", 56 1/2" h. (replaced brasses, imperfections) **$8,050**

Queen Anne Chest Over Drawers

Queen Anne country-style chest over drawers, the rectangular hinged molded top opening above a deep well w/a cast front w/a pair of short over one long false drawers above two working long drawers, applied base molding above the scroll-cut arched apron, old refinish, imperfections, probably Connecticut, mid-18th c., 17 1/2 x 35 1/2", 45" h. (ILLUS.) **$2,070**

Queen Anne tall chest of drawers, tiger stripe maple, the rectangular top w/a narrow flared cornice above a case w/a row of four small thumb-molded drawers over a pair of drawers above four long graduated drawers all w/butterfly brasses & keyhole escutcheons, molded base on tall bracket feet, replaced brasses, old refinish, southeastern New England, ca. 1750, 18 x 34 3/4", 49 1/2" h. (minor imperfections) **$21,850**

Early Southern Sugar Chest

Sugar chest, cherry, a rectangular hinged lid above a deep dovetailed well divided into three compartments, a long bottom drawer w/two turned wood knobs, on baluster-, ring- and knob-turned legs w/knob feet, drawer bottom w/scraps of the "Weekly Courier Journal, Louisville" from the 1880s, refinished, age crack in lid, minor edge damage on feet, Southern, 19th c., 19 1/4 x 27 3/4", 40" h. **$4,675**

Victorian Eastlake Cottage-style Chest

Victorian Eastlake Cottage-style chest of drawers, painted & decorated pine, the super-structure w/a notch-cut crestboard w/peaked center & incised & gilt-trimmed lines & florettes over a gilt-banded frame enclosing a rectangular swivel mirror over decorated panels & a narrow open shelf flanked by shaped side uprights w/gilt-trimmed line-incised florals & loops, the rectangular top w/molded edge w/further gilt trim over a case of four long graduated drawers painted w/a large round continuous reserve decorated w/a lake-side landscape, the reserve surrounded by a rectangular gilt band frame w/angled corners & further stylized gilt florals, on original brown & orange comb-grained ground accented w/black, the top in olive green w/a rose & gold floral design, original round ring pulls & paint, on casters, ca. 1880-90, height loss, 18 3/4 x 38", 76" h. **$978**

Golden Oak Chest of Drawers

Victorian Golden Oak chest of drawers, the top mounted w/a large squared mirror w/rounded corners within a framework w/a high arched & scroll-carved crestrail & shaped sides & rounded bottom corners swiveling between tall scrolled uprights w/scroll carving across the base, the rectangular top w/a serpentine front over a conforming case w/a pair of drawers over two long drawers, all w/pierced brass pulls, simple cabriole front legs & square rear legs, on casters, ca. 1900, 20 x 44", 82" h. **$403**

Rine Renaissance Revival Chest

Victorian Renaissance Revival chest of drawers, walnut & burl walnut, drop-well style, the tall superstructure w/a tall pedimented crest w/carved palmette & scrolls above an arched molded crestrail over a frieze band w/two raised burl panels flanked by scroll-carved brackets on the side panels w/narrow raised burl panels above small candle shelves & tall S-scroll carved brackets all centering a tall mirror, raised side sections w/rectangular white marble tops w/molded edges above stacks of two small drawers flanking the white marble-topped drop well above two long lower drawers w/double raised burl panels centered by cartouche-form carvings & fitted w/brass & wood pulls, canted front corners on base, deep molded flat apron, old refinish, ca. 1870s, 22 x 44", 7' 6" h. **$1,800**

William & Mary chest over drawer, child's, painted pine, a rectangular hinged top w/molded edges opening to a deep well, half-round edge moldings down the corners & above the long base drawer molded to resemble two small drawers, front & sides w/a red painted wash & brown free-hand designs of concentric rings, demi-lune & meandering vines, the drawer painted salmon, red, & brown, single arch molding in black, possibly coastal Massachusetts, early 18th c., 17 1/8 x 28", 19" h. (minor imperfections) **$9,200**

Cupboards

Chippendale Corner Cupboard

Cupboards are storage units. A quick review of early architecture will reinforce that the early settlers were more concerned with putting a roof over their heads than with furniture or styles.

However, even simple cupboards can be broken down into several different types. Many are defined by their usage, such as a linen press or kitchen cupboard.

Within these classifications, many of the cupboards are very stylistic and display elements of a particular period. Wall and corner cupboards often are rather vague in their design, having been crafted for function and often to fit a particular space. The generic term

Pine Jelly Cupboard

"country" serves as a fitting style for many of these cupboards. Few are signed or identified with a specific cabinetmaker. However, types of wood used and other clues help identify the region where they originated and perhaps the time frame.

Often architectural styles dictated how high or wide a cupboard would be, and what kind of materials would be used in its construction. Craftsmen who had a ready supply of poplar used that, while New England furniture makers often used native pine. Cupboards that were made in several different types of wood are commonly found and usually were originally painted or stained to even out their coloration. The term "cupboard door" refers to a simple door created with a flat center section and molded perimeter frame. The term "married" refers to a cupboard where the top and base were combined, sometimes bridging two generations or different time frames.

China Cupboard with Upper Door

China cupboard, Victorian Golden Oak, quarter-sawn oak, a half-round top w/a small scroll-carved crest above a short rectangular bowed glazed door flanked by open shelves backed by small squared beveled mirrors above the half-round case w/a tall glazed bowed center door flanked by curved sides, four wooden shelves & a mirrored back in the upper half, narrow molded base on two short cabriole front legs w/paw feet & shaped rear legs, refinished, ca. 1900, 18 x 48", 6' 4" h. **$2,500**

Chippendale Cherry Corner Cupboard

Corner cupboard, Chippendale, carved cherry, two-part construction: the upper section w/a scrolled molded pediment flanking a fluted keystone w/flame finial above a wide arched door w/geometric glazing flanked by reeded columns, opening to three serpentine-shaped painted shelves; the slightly projecting lower section w/a pair of paneled cupboard doors opening to single shelf flanked by reeded columns, scalloped apron on simple bracket feet, old refinish, hardware changes, minor patching, probably Pennsylvania, early 19th c., 17 3/4 x 41 1/2", 95" h. **$9,200**

Exceptional Country Corner Cupboard

Corner cupboard, country-style, painted pine, two-part construction: the upper section w/a deep coved cornice above a tall 12-pane glazed cupboard door opening to shelves; the lower section w/a mid-molding over a pair of overlapping drawers above a pair of paneled cupboard doors, serpentine apron & high bracket feet, worn original white paint w/vinegar graining in red & yellow ochre, dark grey on apron & feet, one pane replaced, some edge damage & replaced brass knobs, 48 1/2" w., 7' 8 1/2" h. **$19,250**

Large Inlaid Federal Corner Cupboard

Corner cupboard, Federal, cherry, two-part construction: the upper section w/a flat top over a deep coved cornice over a reeded frieze band over a tall 12-pane glazed cupboard door opening to three shelves; the lower section w/mid-molding over a pair of small paneled cupboard doors centered by inlaid rings, molded base on shaped bracket feet, old finish, feet replaced, minor repairs, found in Tennessee, early 19th c., 49 1/2" w., 89 3/4" h. **$5,225**

French Neoclassical Corner Cupboard

Corner cupboard, Neoclassical style, barrel-front hanging-type, mahogany & satinwood inlay, the quarter-round top w/a molded cornice above a pair of tall curved cupboard doors w/a center almond-shaped pinwheel inlay & banded border inlay, on a narrow flat base molding, French polished finish not original, France, ca. 1830, 20 x 26", 44" h. **$850**

Pine Hanging Wall Cupboard

Hanging cupboard, pine, the rectangular top w/a flaring cornice above a conforming case w/a paneled door opening to a shelved interior, over a molding above a shelf w/shaped sides, red-stained, 19th c., 9 1/4 x 20", 25 1/2" h. **$978**

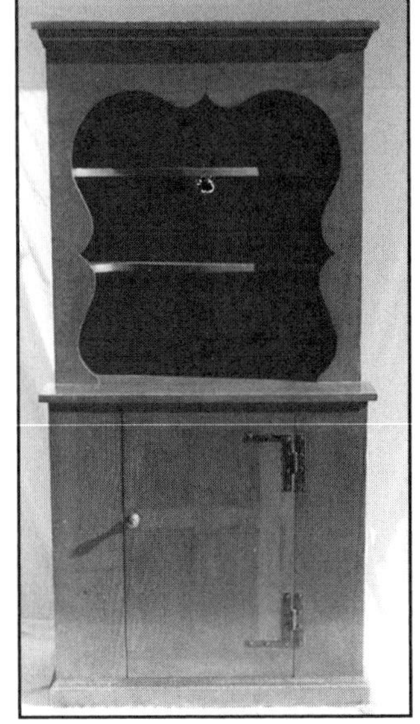

Nutting Pine Hutch Cupboard

Hutch cupboard, Wallace Nuttting-signed, pine, one-piece construction, the rectangular top w/a wide stepped cornice above a scallop-cut open top enclosing two shaped shelves above the stepped out lower case w/a single flat cupboard door w/HL hinges, Model No. 923 Pine Scrolled Cupboard, early 20th c. (ILLUS.) **$4,290**

Jelly cupboard, painted, a high peaked crestboard on the rectangular top over a pair of drawers over a pair of tall paneled doors w/iron latches, simple bracket feet & bootjack ends, old dry mustard yellow paint, found in Berks County, Pennsylvania, 19th c., 17 x 44 1/2", 4' 10 1/4" h. **$3,630**

Paint-decorated Jelly Cupboard

Jelly cupboard, country-style, painted & decorated pine & poplar, the rectangular top w/a three-quarters gallery w/rounded ends above a pair of molded drawers w/large wood knobs overhanging a pair of baluster- and acorn-turned short side drops above a pair of tall paneled doors, scalloped apron & ring- and knob-turned feet, old brownish yellow wood graining w/burl design on drawers & door panels, Pennsylvania, mid-19th c., 24 1/2 x 46 3/4", overall 58 3/4" h. (ILLUS.) **$495**

Jelly cupboard, painted pine & poplar, rectangular top w/high three-quarter gallery w/shaped ends, a pair of drawers w/old replaced wooden knobs above a pair of tall paneled cupboard doors w/old brass latches, one-board ends w/cut-out feet, found

Golden Oak Kitchen Cupboard

in Smoketown, Pennsylvania, old yellow graining over red, 19th c., 13 x 40", overall 47 1/2" h. **$3,960**

Kitchen cupboard, Golden Oak, two-piece construction: the upper section w/a rectangular top w/stepped cornice above a pair of single-pane glazed doors opening to two shelves above a row of drawers w/a long drawer flanked by two small drawers; the lower section w/a cylinder front w/a pull-out work shelf over a tall paneled-front fold-down flour bin beside a square double-paneled door over a drawer, scrolled bracket feet, on casters, ca. 1900, 21 x 37 1/2", 83" h. (ILLUS.) **$1,320**

Fine Classical Linen Press

Linen press, Classical, carved walnut veneer, the rectangular top above a plain frieze band over two tall recessed three-panel doors flanked by wide carved & fluted flat columns on molded bases above four front ring-turned legs w/knob feet, the front doors open to an interior of shelves & drawers, the central ones small & veneered, the recessed panel sides open to an interior w/wooden pegs, old surface, minor imperfections, probably Philadelphia, ca. 1830, 24 x 84", 87 1/2" h. **$10,925**

Early Ohio Pewter Cupboard

Pewter cupboard, country-style, poplar, one-piece construction, a rectangular top w/a widely flaring stepped cornice above a tall beaded open hutch w/three shelves above a stepped-out lower case w/a single cupboard door w/four raised panels, old red finish, attributed to Ohio, cornice replaced, early 19th c., top 14 x 39 1/4", 79" h. (ILLUS.) **$3,960**

Pie safe, cherry & punched tin, a rectangular top above a pair of drawers w/simple turned knobs above a pair of large cupboard doors each w/four large rectangular punched tin panels decorated w/a central pinwheel w/fanned leaf devices in each corner, flat

Fine Cherry & Tin Pie Safe

base, baluster- and ring-turned legs w/peg feet, old worn brown finish w/traces of oilcloth, two punched tin panels on each end, found in east Tennessee, mid-19th c., 18 3/4 x 53", 49" h. (ILLUS.) **$5,225**

Pie safe, painted cherry, a rectangular top above a pair of dovetailed drawers over a pair of tall cupboard doors each fitted w/six side-by-side punched tin panels forming continuous patterns of central rings enclosing four hearts & half-round & quarter-round corner rings w/hearts alternating w/a large rounded pinwheel in each panel, side tin panels w/pinwheel & birds designs, a flat apron & round ring-turned legs w/knob feet, old green repaint, square nail & peg construction, 24 1/2 x 58", 64" h. (door hinges, pulls & turn buckles old replacements) **$4,675**

Mid-Atlantic Federal Cupboard

Pie safe, painted poplar, a rectangular top above a pair of tall cupboard doors each fitted w/three pierced tin panels decorated w/a large five-point star within a circle in the center against an urn device in background, two small stars in the upper panel corners & two larger ones in the lower corners, three tin panels down each side, on tall square stile legs, old black repaint, white porcelain door knob, tins mounted backward, 19th c., 17 x 41 1/2", 59" h. (one side tin starting to deteriorate, one door w/small half moon edge cut-out) **$2,090**

Step-back wall cupboard, Federal, maple, two-part construction: the upper section w/a rectangular top & deep flared cornice above two 6-pane glazed cupboard doors flanking a 3-panel central panel above a tall pie shelf w/scalloped sides; the stepped-out lower section w/a pair of narrow long drawers flanking a small central drawer over a pair of paneled cupboard doors, molded base w/serpentine apron & simple bracket feet, Mid-Atlantic States, early 19th c., H-hinges on upper doors, 17 1/2 x 57 1/2", 84" h. (ILLUS.) **$6,325**

Step-back wall cupboard, Federal style, pine, two-part construction: the upper section w/a rectangular top w/a deep stepped flaring cornice over a patterned diagonally-reeded frieze band above a pair of 6-pane glazed doors w/arched top panes & molded muntins all flanked by paneled & reeded pilasters; the lower section w/a mid-molding on the projecting top over a long molded central drawer flanked by small square end drawers above a pair of double-molded cupboard doors flanked by tall narrow molded panels, molded base on slender arched feet, old brass pulls, old refinish, probably Hackensack, New Jersey, ca. 1810, 19 x 50 3/4", 85" h. **$10,350**

Step-back wall cupboard, Georgian, walnut, two-piece construction: the upper section w/a rectangular top over a narrow flared cornice & a carved dentil band above a pair of 6-pane glazed cupboard doors flanking three central fixed panes all flanked by side rails w/a carved paterae panel above a row of three small raised rectangular panels over an open pie shelf w/scroll-cut brackets; the projecting lower section w/a pair of drawers w/small wood knobs flanked by horizontally incised rectangular panels over a pair of raised panel cupboard doors flanked by long narrow raised panels, molded base on scroll-cut bracket feet, old dark varnish finish, Canada, early 19th c., 12 1/2 x 63", 85 1/4" h. (restoration to top, back replaced by plywood) **$4,400**

Early Pennsylvania Painted Cupboard

Step-back wall cupboard, painted pine, two-part construction: the upper section w/a rectangular top & deep flaring cornice above a pair of 6-pane glazed cupboard doors opening to three shelves w/plate grooves & spoon rack above a low open pie shelf; the stepped-out lower section w/a row of three drawers above a pair of paneled cupboard doors, molded base & simple bracket feet, later off-white paint, replaced hardware, Pennsylvania, late 18th c., imperfections, 17 1/2 x 52", 84" h. **$9,775**

Ornately Carved Baroque Cupboard

Step-back wall cupboard, Victorian Baroque Revival substyle, carved oak, two-part construction: the upper section w/a rectangular top w/a high ornately-cut crestrail centered by a carved grotesque mask of Bacchus clenching grapevines in his teeth which scroll across the front of the crestrail, above a deep stepped & flaring cornice above a frieze band carved w/grapevine & centered by a scroll-carved mount, all above a pair of tall glazed cupboard doors w/narrow beaded molding flanked by fruit- and leaf-carved side rails, the stepped-out lower section w/a molded edge above a pair of drawers carved w/scrolling grapevines over a pair of paneled cupboard doors bordered by beaded molding & carved in bold relief w/figural tavern scenes, further fruit & leaf carving down the sides, carved flaring flat base molding on bun feet, refinished, Europe, late 19th c., 22 x 44", 8' 4" h. **$3,400**

Victorian Country Step-Back Cupboard

Step-back wall cupboard, Victorian country-style, pine, two-piece construction: the upper section w/a rectangular top w/angled front corners over a deep stepped & flaring cornice over a frieze band of carved arrow-head devices separated by three half-round drop spindles over a pair of 4-pane glazed cupboard doors w/thumb latches & small half-round spindles applied to dividing rails above a pair of small drawers w/raised panels separated w/applied low pyramidal blocks; the stepped-out lower section w/a pair of double-paneled cupboard doors w/a small button in the center of each panel & cast-iron latches, flanked at the sides by chamfered corners w/half-round applied spindles, flat molded apron on bracket feet, refinished, ca. 1860, 23 x 58", 7' 1" h. **$4,500**

Step-back wall cupboard, Victorian country-style, walnut, two-part construction: the upper section w/a rectangular top & deep flaring flat cornice above a pair of tall paneled cupboard doors w/cast-iron latches w/porcelain knobs above a pie shelf w/shaped sides; the lower stepped-out section w/a pair of drawers w/porcelain knobs over a pair of paneled cupboard doors w/cast-iron latches, simple bracket feet, mellow finish, 19th c., 18 x 45", 85 1/2" h. (one knob missing, right door swollen) **$2,090**

Step-back wall cupboard, walnut, two-part construction: the upper section w/an overhanging flared & stepped cornice above a pair of 6-pane glazed cupboard doors opening to two shelves fitted w/spoon racks, flanked by wide fluted pilasters over the open pie shelf; the stepped-out lower section w/fluted side pilasters flanking a row of three small drawers each separated by a fluted block above a pair of wide paneled cupboard doors centered by another fluted pilaster, molded base on straight bracket feet, old finish, Pennsylvania, 1750-70, 19 1/2 x 63 1/2", 90" h. (patch on left side of cornice, strips added to base of upper section) **$20,700**

Step-back wall cupboard, walnut & poplar, two-piece construction: the upper section w/a rectangular top over a flat angled cornice over a pair of very tall paneled doors over a low pie shelf; the lower stepped-out section w/a pair of drawers w/wooden knobs over a pair of paneled cupboard doors, simple bracket feet, bootjack sides, old refinish, mid-19th c., 19 x 45", 85 3/4" h. (chip on rear foot, one end of cornice replaced) **$1,870**

Fancy Oak Step-Back Wall Cupboard

Step-back wall cupboard, Victorian Golden Oak sub-style, two-part construction: the upper section w/a high serpentine & scroll-carved front crestrail above a egg-and-dart molding above a pair of glazed cupboard doors w/shaped tops trimmed w/carved scrolls & opening to two shelves; the lower section w/a rectangular support shelf raised on S-scroll brackets & a paneled back on the rectangular top w/molded edges above a pair of drawers w/stamped brass pulls over a single long drawer all flanked by sunbursts & diamond carving above a pair of large paneled cupboard doors w/bold scroll-carved designs, serpentine apron & bracket feet, refinished, ca. 1900, 18 x 42", 7' 8" h. **$3,600**

Eighteenth Century Wall Cupboard

Wall cupboard, Chippendale country-style, painted pine, one-piece construction, a rectangular top w/narrow flared cornice above a pair of tall narrow doors each w/two narrow raised panels & mounted w/H-hinges, molded base w/short bracket feet, opens to five shelves, old tan over green paint, hinges appear to be original, probably Rhode Island, late 18th c., imperfections, 10 1/2 x 41 3/4", 75 3/4" h. **$6,900**

Unique Classical Open Cupboard

Wall cupboard, Classical, painted & decorated, a rectangular top w/flared & stepped cornice above a tall open compartment w/seven shelves flanked by tall tapering pilasters w/carved, scrolled Ionic capitals, painted to resemble rosewood, probably New England, ca. 1820-30, minor imperfections, 11 1/2 x 32", 65 1/2" h. **$5,463**

Short Cherry Wall Cupboard

Wall cupboard, country-style, cherry, one-piece construction, a rectangular top above a single 4-pane glazed cupboard door above a raised-panel cupboard door both flanked by wide side boards, old brass hardware & latches, refinished, scalloped apron, 19th c., top 13 1/2 x 32", 54 1/2" h. **$1,870**

Fancy Federal Pine Wall Cupboard

Wall cupboard, Federal, pine, one-piece construction, the rectangular top w/deep stepped cornice & blocked corners above a conforming case w/a pair of tall geometrically-glazed cupboard doors flanked by wide reeded pilasters & opening to interior reeded columns & arched top shelved unit above a mid-molding over a pair of paneled cupboard doors above further reeded pilasters ending in a blocked deep base, old mellow refinishing, base molding replaced, some height loss & restoration, early 19th c., 15 x 42 1/2", 76" h. **$2,750**

Gothic Revival Oak Wall Cupboard

Wall cupboard, late Victorian Gothic Revival, quarter-sawn oak, a high ornately pierce-carved crest centered by a chalice overflowing w/grapevines continuing down the side of the crest, the flaring crestrail w/sawtooth carving above a single glazed door w/carved trefoils in the upper corners above a glazed arched panel w/Gothic arch muntins centered by a carved rose wreath, sawtooth bands down the sides & at the base above a single drawer w/a wooden knob, simple molded base, probably used for storing wine & hosts in a Roman Catholic church, original finish, ca. 1900, 12 x 21", 34" h. **$950**

Late European Welsh Cupboard

Welsh cupboard, pine & poplar, two-part construction: the upper section w/a rectangular top w/a deep flared cornice above a large three-shelved open compartment w/a scalloped top rail & sides; the stepped-out lower section w/a fold-out work surface above a case w/a row of three drawers over a square cupboard door beside two long drawers all w/turned wood knobs, flat base w/narrow molding, raised on bun feet on pegs, waxed finish, Europe, ca. 1910, 24 x 60", 6' 10" h. **$1,400**

Desks

Slant Front Chippendale Desk

A desk is a furniture form that appears throughout most of the furniture styles. Functioning as a command center for early households, a well-appointed desk served as a place to organize finances, write letters, and keep track of important documents. The furniture craftsmen who created these masterpieces used some ordinary wood as well as more exotic wood, such as bird's-eye maple. Use of inlays helped exhibit wealth and style.

The term "slant front" or "slant lid" describes the flat writing surface that folds down from the top to a comfortable writing height. By closing the front and perhaps locking it, important papers could be secured. Secret compartments and drawers were also built into some desks.

Walnut Roll-top Desk

A "fall front" denotes a board that lowers from the top to a writing surface; it may or may not fit on a slant like a slant front. Some fall fronts, especially in the Arts & Crafts era and on butler's desks, were not slanted.

A "knee hole" desk refers to a desk with a flat working surface, usually supported by two banks (or piers) of drawers or legs, allowing the user to sit with his or her knees under the desk top.

A "lady's desk" is usually more diminutive and allowed a lady to sit with her legs under the working surface. She also had some compartments at her disposal, but often not as many as on a slant front desk. A "Davenport" is often a smaller version with fold-out working surfaces.

A "butler's" desk is generally a smaller writing surface with fewer interior compartments. The butler was probably using the desk for simple record keeping or perhaps only writing instructions to others and not using the space for long correspondence.

When purchasing an antique desk, look for signs of wear, and pull out the slant front supports and see if the front rests flat on them. Look for signs of replaced hardware by examining the interior of drawers. Any holes not being used for current hardware may be a clue to the location of earlier hardware. Check to see if the height of the writing surface is comfortable. Perhaps the feet have been altered; check them carefully too. If purchasing a rolltop or tambour closing desk, check to see that the top moves easily. Any leather- or felt-covered surfaces should show some signs of wear. It is not unusual to find some repairs or restorations to early desks. Adjustments to the value of a particular desk will be determined by these factors, as well as by the style, coloration, and overall appeal to the buyer.

Also see Secretaries.

Fine Art Deco Walnut Desk

Art Deco desk, walnut & ivory, the rectangular top w/rounded corners & inset front section decorated w/veneer panels & inlaid banding above the shallow case w/a pair of small drawers w/square ivory pulls on each side of a long central drawer over a thin pull-out slide, outset slender rounded tapering legs w/light stripe inlay, designed by Joubert et Petit, produced by D.I.M., France, ca. 1925, 43 1/2" l., 32" h. **$14,950**

"Bonheur du Jour" Desk

Art Nouveau "bonheur du jour" desk, fruitwood marquetry, central upright case w/fall front opening to an interior fitted w/shelves, pigeonholes, pen tray & glass Waterman inkwell, above a writing plateau w/drawer below, all inlaid w/various woods w/stylized poppies & leafage, the whole raised on tapering legs carved w/poppies, signed in marquetry "Galle/Nancy," ca. 1900, 21 x 28 1/2 x 46" **$5,750**

Chippendale Slant Front Desk

Chippendale slant front desk, carved maple & cherry, a narrow rectangular top above a hinged molded slant lid opening to an interior fitted w/a central fan-carved drawer flanked by document drawers & six pigeonholes above four short drawers, the case below w/four long graduated drawers above a central apron pendant, scroll-cut bracket feet, repairs to feet, New England, probably New Hampshire, ca. 1780, 17 1/2 x 35", 41 3/4" h. **$6,900**

Classical Butler's Desk

Classical butler's desk, carved mahogany & mahogany veneer, the rectangular top above a drawer opening to a writing surface & a bird's-eye maple interior of eight drawers & six valanced pigeonholes, the case w/three recessed long drawers w/flanking free-standing columns w/acanthus carved Corinthian capitals, on a stepped plinth base & large ball- turned feet on casters, replaced brasses, old feet, possibly New England, ca. 1825, imperfections, 22 x 45", 48" h. **$920**

Colonial Revival Lady's Desk

Colonial Revival lady's writing desk, quarter-sawn oak, the scalloped & scroll-carved crestrail over a narrow shelf above the wide hinged slant front decorated w/applied delicate scrolling & opening to a fitted interior w/pigeonholes, small drawers & the fold-down writing surface, the serpentine lower case w/a long conforming top drawer over a pair of small drawers flanking the bracket-trimmed kneehole opening, raised on slender simple cabriole front legs, original pierced brass hardware, refinished, ca. 1910, 18 x 32", 44" h. **$1,200**

Country-style Plantation Desk

Country-style plantation desk, butternut, two-part construction: the tall upper section w/a rectangular top w/deep stepped & flaring cornice above an open-fronted case w/32 pigeonholes above vertical slots flanking a galleried central compartment over a pair of drawers; the stepped-out lower section w/a rectangular top over a single long drawer w/carved pulls, on ring-, knob- and baluster-turned legs w/knob feet, long oval raised molding at the sides of the upper case, ca. 1860-70, 26 x 38", 6' 8" h. **$750**

Fine Federal Lady's Desk

Federal lady's desk, mahogany & mahogany veneer, two-part construction: the upper section w/a rectangular top w/a narrow molded cornice over a pair of beaded & veneered cupboard doors enclosing three shaped document drawers flanked by two short drawers above three valanced compartments; the lower projecting section w/a fold-out writing surface above a case w/three long cockbeaded & veneered drawers, scalloped apron & ring- and baluster-turned legs w/peg feet, old pressed glass pulls, old refinish, imperfec-tions, Massachusetts, ca. 1810, 32 3/4 x 39 1/2", 53" h. **$3,220**

George III-Style Partner's Desk

Federal "tambour" desk, inlaid mahogany, two-part construction: the upper section w/a stepped-back rectangular top above a row of two long drawers flanking a short center drawer all above twin tambour doors flanking a small plain prospect door all opening to an arrangement of drawers & valanced pigeonholes; the lower section stepped-out w/a fold-down writing surface over a case of three long graduated drawers flanked by banded stiles & raised on ring- and rod-turned tapering cylindrical legs w/peg feet, probably Newburyport, Massachusetts, early 19th c., 21 1/2 x 40 3/4", 52" h. **$4,140**

George III-Style partner's desk, mahogany, the rectangular molded top inset w/gilt-tooled burgundy leather, above an apron fitted w/three drawers on each side, raised on cabriole legs w/scroll-carved knees & ending in claw-and-ball feet, England, early 20th c., 36 x 61 1/2", 31" h. (ILLUS.) **$3,220**

Louis XV-Style Cylinder-front Desk

Louis XV-Style cylinder-front desk, gilt-bronze mounted mahogany, a rectangular top w/a low gilt-metal gallery above three narrow drawers w/gilt-bronze pulls & mounts above the wide cylinder front w/gilt-bronze scroll banding opening to a slide-out inset leather writing surface, all above a heavy gilt-bronze border over the apron w/a long central drawer w/gilt-bronze mounts flanked on one side by two small drawers & on the other by a single deep drawer each w/scrolling gilt-bronze mounts, on simple cabriole legs w/long gilt-bronze scroll mounts down the legs ending in feet w/sabots, France, late 19th c., 30 x 64", 48" h. **$13,800**

Lifetime Mission Slant Front Desk

Mission-style (Arts & Crafts movement) slant front desk, oak, a low crestrail on a narrow top shelf over the wide hinged slant front opening to a fitted interior including drawers above a deep apron w/a pair of small, deep drawers flanking a small, arched central kneehole drawer, square legs extending above the top of the front edge, low side stretchers joined by a narrow medial shelf stretcher, new dark finish, foil decal of the Lifetime Furniture Company, 16 x 31 1/2", 44 1/2" h. **$1,045**

Herman Miller 1950s Desk

Modern style desk, walnut & brass, a demi-lune shaped top above a conforming case w/a three-slot compartment above a stack of two drawers w/round brass pulls & open side compartment to the left of the kneehole, raised on cylindrical brass legs, design attributed to Gilbert Rhode, manufactured by Herman Miller, Zeeland, Michigan, ca. 1950s, minor wear, 24 x 45 1/2", 29 1/4" h. (ILLUS.) **$1,150**

Plantation desk, country-style, painted poplar, two-part construction: the upper section w/a rectangular top w/a flat flared cornice above a single wide 6-pane glazed cupboard door opening to a shelf above a high arched base opening; the widely stepped-out lower section w/a long front hinged drop leaf w/rounded corners, raised on square tapering legs, old worn red finish, 19th c., base 17 1/2 x 36 1/4", 66 1/2" h. **$550**

Queen Anne-Style Library Desk

Queen Anne-Style library desk, oak, a wide rectangular top w/molded edge above a deep bowed band w/a long conforming drawer w/bail pulls at the front above the kneehole opening, above an incurved band w/a small drawer on each side of the kneehole, raised on heavy cabriole legs ending in paw feet, ca. 1900, 28 x 45", 30" h. (ILLUS.) **$863**

Schoolmaster's desk on frame, poplar, two-part construction: the upper section w/a narrow top shelf w/a three-quarters gallery above a wide hinged sloping lid opening to the dovetailed case w/ten pigeonholes; the lower section w/a single long drawer w/two wooden knobs raised on baluster- and ring-turned legs w/knob feet joined by flat box stretchers, original red wash, 19th c., 26 1/2 x 39" x 47 1/2" (base wobbly). **$660**

Aesthetic Movement Captain's Desk

Victorian Aesthetic Movement captain's desk, walnut & burl walnut, the superstructure w/a high peaked center crest topped by a short spindled gallery over a sloped shingle-like roof projecting above a band of ebonized scallops & flanked by small open shelves w/scallop-cut aprons raised on block- and ring-turned columnar supports flanking a projecting small central compartment w/a beveled mirror in the door flanked by side panels decorated w/incised & ebonized geometric incised lines, a wide hinged slope front writing surface opening to a fitted well above a line-incised & ebonized front apron projecting above the lower case & supported by ring-, knob- and

Ornate Baroque Revival Partner's Desk

rob-turned slender spindles flanking a pair of paneled doors decorated w/burl & gilt-incised line decoration, original finish, ca. 1880, 22 x 30", 4' 2" h. **$2,000**

Victorian Baroque Revival partner's desk, oak & oak veneer, the long oval top w/molded flaring edges above rounded end sections each w/a pair of drawers centering ornately scroll-carved curved doors centering on each side a long scroll-carved drawer over the kneehole opening, raised on a scroll-carved apron & four heavy animal paw legs on casters, late 19th c. **$3,575**

Victorian Cylinder-front Desk

Victorian cylinder-front desk, Renaissance Revival substyle, walnut, a narrow molded top above the high cylinder-front w/recessed burl panels opening to an interior fitted w/large pigeonholes over small drawers above a mid-molding over the lower case w/an arched central long drawer over a paneled kneehole opening flanked by a pair of projecting drawers w/recessed burl panels above stacks of three drawers w/recessed burl panels flanked by molded & shaped blocks, paneled base ends, plinth base, right side w/side-lock false drawer, kneehole w/false privacy panel w/locking door, ca. 1880, 31 x 48", 56" h. **$2,588**

Country Eastlake Captain's Desk

Victorian Eastlake country-style captain's desk, walnut, the superstructure w/an arched, pierced & scroll-cut crestrail flanked by pointed side rails over the narrow shelf above a lower open shelf flanked by pierced, arched sides above a small line-inlaid drawer flanking an open compartment, the slant-front case w/a wide lid opening to a well & w/a small candle shelf to one side, raised on pierce-carved cross-form supports joined by a ring- and baluster-turned cross stretcher w/a small turned finial, original finish, ca. 1875-85, 24 x 30", 42" h. **$650**

William & Mary Desk on Frame

William & Mary desk on frame, tulipwood & oak, two-part construction: the upper section w/a narrow rectangular top over a hinged raised-panel fall-front opening to an interior of four compartments, three drawers & a well w/sliding closure above a double arched deep molded front; the lower section w/a mid-molding above a wide molded rectangular top overhanging a deep apron w/a long drawer w/brass teardrop pulls & a diamond-form key-hole escutcheon over the valanced apron, knob- and trumpet-turned legs on shaped flat cross stretchers over turned turnip feet, replaced brasses, old refinish, minor imperfec-tions, probably Connecticut, early 18th c., 15 x 24 3/4", 42 1/2" h. .. **$17,250**

Hall Furnishings

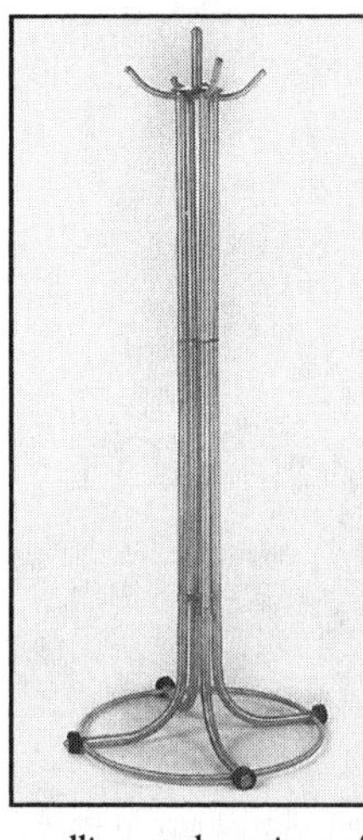

Early Aluminum Hall Rack

Hall furnishings include all the types of furniture that were made to be used exclusively in a hallway setting. Benches, chairs, hat racks, and hall trees all offered comfort or a place to put coats and hats.

Like many other pieces of furniture designed for a specific use, some hall furnishings do not fall neatly into any one furniture period.

Hallways in great American manor houses were often gathering places for guests. When "calling," it was customary to be received in a spacious hall, where one's card would be placed in a calling card receiver, often held on a side table. Perhaps a coat or hat were taken to be hung up. A chair or bench was offered for the waiting visitor, or perhaps they were taken to a parlor to wait.

Hallways in later homes, such as those designed in the Victorian era or the Arts & Crafts era, were destined to serve as an area to prepare to go out into the cold. Benches were used to put on one's boots, and seats held storage areas for hats and gloves. The foyers in today's homes are small compared to the spacious areas of earlier architectural styles.

Oak Hall Tree with Mirror over Roundel

Even the simplest of halls usually included a place to hang a coat. Such furnishings are often called clothes trees, which describes their spindly appearance. Costumer, the name given by the original Arts & Crafts period designers, is another name given to the clothes tree. A coat rack generally has larger hooks and is more substantial to bear the weight of coats.

A hall bench usually has a place to sit while putting on outerware, and many also contain a storage area. A hall chair is a chair with a wide seat, usually substantial in form.

Most halls included a mirror, some large and others more in scale with the rest of the furniture of the hall. It is important to remember that the homeowner was trying to impress a visitor with the grand nature of his furnishings, and the hall was often the place where first impressions were made. A well-proportioned mirror was an excellent way to subtly display one's good taste and sense of style.

Only items specifically designed for use in a hall are included in this section. Refer to specific sections for other types of benches, chairs, mirrors, stands, and tables that may have also been used in a hallway.

Carved Golden Oak Hall Rack

Hall rack, Victorian Golden Oak, wall-mounted, wide flat upper & lower quarter-sawn oak rails w/ornate leafy scroll carving joined to slender ring-turned side stiles w/knob finials & mounted w/three double brass hooks on each side, a central rectangular beveled mirror joined by short carved rails to the side stiles, refinished, ca. 1890, 44" l., 36" h. **$650**

Impressive Golden Oak Hall Tree

Hall tree, Victorian Golden Oak style, quarter-sawn oak, the tall back w/an arched crestrail centered w/a pointed scroll-carved finial & a wide band of raised scrolls above a tall rectangular beveled mirror w/scalloped top flanked by side columns on leaf scrolls, mounted w/four cast-brass coat hooks above a plain back panel flanked by shaped flat open arms over the rectangular hinged lift seat over a deep well & apron w/a serpentine edge, shaped arm supports form the front legs, refinished, ca. 1900, 20 x 28", 7' h. **$1,600**

Highboys & Lowboys

Chippendale Highboy

The highboy, a popular style of chests of drawers, was first popularized in England. However, it did not take long for American craftsmen to start designing and creating exquisite examples of impressive chests of drawers. As the name implies, the chest towers to the ceiling, some with high bonnets and decorative cresting, while others have flat tops with decorative moldings. The bases usually contain additional drawers and are raised up on legs that help determine the furniture style. Like well-made desks and secretaries, some highboys have been found to be hiding secret compartments.

Other names for highboys include chest on frame and chest over drawers. Before purchasing a highboy, carefully examine it. Pull

Queen Anne Lowboy

out all the drawers and see that all the dovetailing is exactly the same. Drawers should move in and out smoothly. Allow for some shrinkage of the wood and wear through the years. Check to see if all the brasses are of the same period.

A lowboy is best thought of as a companion to a highboy but smaller in scale. Expect to find the same stylistic characteristics as those found on highboys, i.e., claw and ball feet on Chippendale examples. As architecture dictated some forms of furniture, clothing styles also changed, and that affected how furniture was used too. A lowboy offered storage for necessities such as gloves, hose, and smaller articles of clothing.

Connecticut Queen Anne Highboy

Queen Anne bonnet-top highboy, cherry, two-part construction: the upper section w/a broken-scroll crest w/three tall slender urn-form finials above a deep fan-carved drawer flanked by short drawers above a stack of four long graduated drawers w/pierced butterfly brasses; the lower section w/a mid-molding over a long narrow drawer over a fan-carved center drawer flanked by smaller drawers, scalloped apron, simple cabriole legs ending in raised pad feet, Connecticut, late 18th c., some original brasses, old refinish, some reconstruction, 22 x 40", 7' h. **$9,500**

Fine Queen Anne Maple Highboy

Queen Anne flat-top highboy, maple, two-part construction: the upper section w/a rectangular top over a deep coved cornice over a row of three drawers w/the center one fan-carved over a stack of four long graduated thumb-molded drawers; the lower section w/a mid-molding over a long drawer over three deep drawers w/the center one fan-carved, scalloped apron & cabriole legs ending in pad feet on platforms, the butterfly brasses appear to be original, old refinish, minor imperfections, Massachusetts, ca. 1760, 20 1/4 x 38 1/2", 74 1/2" h. **$27,600**

Rare William & Mary Highboy

William & Mary flat-top highboy, maple & pine, two-part construction: the upper section w/a rectangular flat top w/narrow flaring cornice over a row of three small drawers over three long graduated drawers; the lower section w/a heavy mid-molding over a case w/two deep drawers flanking a shallow central drawer over a triple-arched apron, raised on four trumpet-form front legs w/bun feet joined by flat curved stretchers, grained in the late 19th c., original brasses & keyhole escutcheons, North Shore, Massachusetts, 1700-30, minor repairs to stretchers, 22 5/8 x 44", 63 1/2" h. **$34,500**

Queen Anne Lowboy

Queen Anne lowboy, mahogany, a rectangular top w/molded edges above a single long drawer w/three large butterfly brasses over a row of three drawers w/the central one fan-carved, scalloped apron w/two teardrop drops, cabriole legs ending in pad feet, New England, 18th c., 20 x 30", 30" h. **$4,600**

William & Mary-Style Lowboy

William & Mary-Style lowboy, cherry & mahogany, the rectangular top w/molded edge overhanging a case w/a pair of deep drawers flanking a shallow center drawer, deeply scalloped apron raised on four trumpet-form legs resting on a serpentine cross-stretcher on turned turnip feet, original brass teardrop pulls, original finish, ca. 1880, 20 x 30", 30" h. **$600**

Mirrors

Federal Wall Mirror

Mirror, mirror on the wall—what an important part of furnishings mirrors play in our lives.

All furniture periods have included mirrors, and as the manufacturing techniques improved, sizes expanded, too. It is usually acceptable for an antique mirror to show some signs of aging, loss of silvering, etc. While mirrors are commonly used to view one's image, they are also important decorative elements. Used to create the illusion of more spacious appearances, they also capture light and reflect it back into a room.

Some mirror-related terms:

Architectural—usually combines architectural elements of the design period, used to reflect light.

Cheval—large mirrors that are designed with a base and also can be used in a free-standing position.

Dressing—used to view one's appearance, sometimes mounted on a base or used on a tabletop.

Aesthetic Movement Pier Mirror

Eglomise—a type of painting on glass where the design is painted on the back and intended to be viewed through the glass.

Girandole—circular convex mirror.

Looking Glass—a small mirror used to view one's image.

Over Mantel—large mirrors used over a fireplace mantel, primarily used to reflect light into a room.

Pier—large mirror either hung over a pier table or hung at a level so one could view skirts and feet.

Scroll—a scrolled mirror frame, made to be hung on a wall.

Shaving—used to view one's appearance while shaving. Usually found on bases, sometimes with small drawers to holding accessories.

Wall—a mirror designed to be hung on the wall and used for either viewing of one's image or reflecting light.

Art Nouveau-Style Mirror

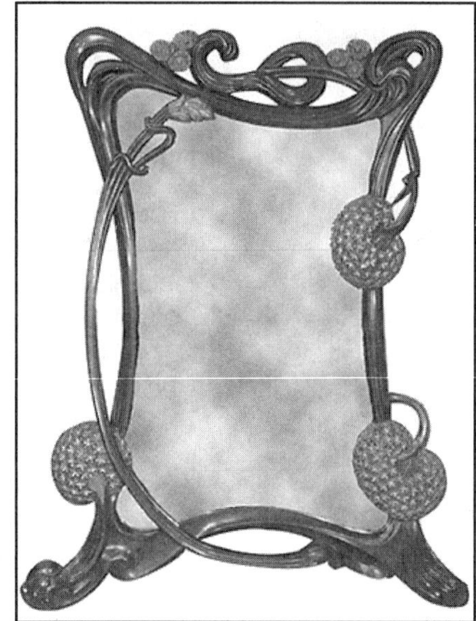

Art Nouveau-Style wall mirror, carved mahogany, the rectilinear form of pierced whiplashes w/gilded blossom clusters surrounding the conforming mirror, some age but not period, age cracks, old finish, 38 x 47 1/2" **$715**

Fine Chippendale Mirror with Phoenix

Chippendale wall mirror, mahogany, the arched & scroll-cut crest centering a pierced & gilded carved phoenix flanked by scrolled ears above a rectangular & gilt-carved liner w/cusped upper corners enclosing a mirror, scroll-shaped base, American or English, late 18th c., 20 1/4 x 36 1/2" **$4,025**

Classical Giltwood Pier Mirror

Classical pier mirror, giltwood, the rectangular divided mirror plate surrounded by flattened & partially reeded pilasters w/bold carved fleur-de-lis corner mounts, second quarter 19th c., 34 1/2 x 62" **$2,300**

Fine Classical Shaving Mirror

Classical shaving mirror, mahogany & mahogany veneer, table-top, a flat crest cornice raised on half-round columnar supports flanking the swiveling rectangular mirror w/rounded frame, above a rectangular top w/rounded front corners over two ogee-fronted drawers w/an ivory keyhole or tiny knob, original finish, ca. 1840, 10 x 16", 28" h. **$350**

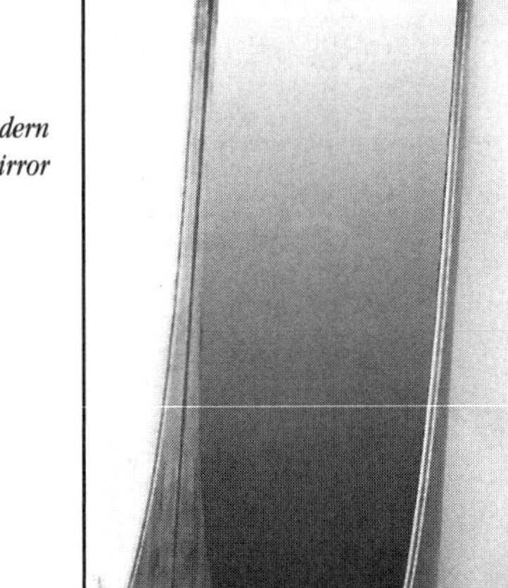

Danish Modern Wall Mirror

Danish Modern wall mirror, walnut, a flat crestrail above flaring shaped & molded narrow sides w/a narrow shelf below the tall mirror plate, Denmark, ca. 1955, 17 1/4" w., 24 3/4" h. **$201**

Fine Empire Revival Cheval Mirror

Empire Revival cheval mirror, ormolu mounted mahogany, a long oval narrow frame w/ormolu mounts enclosing a beveled mirror swiveling between tall square uprights w/urn-form finials & swelled scroll base bracket all decorated w/ormolu mounts, the uprights also w/heavy scrolled inner brackets w/ormolu mounts resting on the heavy bottom cross stretcher w/long ornate ormolu mounts, raised on heavy rectangular blocks raised on bun feet on casters, original finish, ca. 1880, 36" w., 6' 10" h. .... **$3,000-$3,500**

Federal Mahogany Dressing Mirror

Federal dressing mirror, mahogany & mahogany veneer, the shield-form mirror in a conforming veneered frame w/string-inlaid edges flanked by scrolled & incised supports w/ringed bosses at the terminals, on stepped & shaped trestle feet joined by incised shaped stretcher, old finish, imperfections, label of I. Richman, New York City, late 18th - early 19th c., 8 3/4 x 14", 21 1/4" h. **$1,265**

George III-Style Girandole Mirror

George III-Style girandole mirrors, giltwood, a round mirror plate within a molded frame surmounted by a spread-winged eagle & scrolling leafy vines, the similar apron fitted w/a pair of candlearms, chips & losses, England, late 19th c., 20 x 34 1/2", pr. (ILLUS. of one) **$4,312**

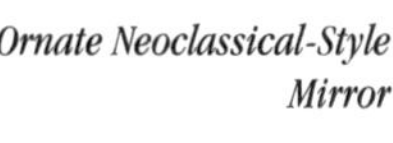

Ornate Neoclassical-Style Mirror

Neoclassical-Style wall mirror, carved mahogany, an oval frame carved w/resembled clustered, wrapped reeds w/a pair of figural carved kissing birds at the top above a floral-carved swag, suspended on a long forked branch w/a large bow at the top, further floral-carved swags along the lower frame, ca. 1920s, 22 x 40" **$850**

Etched Queen Anne Mirror

Queen Anne wall mirror, walnut, the shaped crest centering an upper mirror plate etched w/flowers issuing from a vase flanked by birds & smaller vases issuing flowers surmounted by a scrolling foliate border, a lower rectangular beveled mirror w/conforming frame, American or English, 1740-60, 17 x 35 1/4" **$3,220**

Fine Regency Girandole Mirror

Regency girandole mirror, gilt gesso, the round convex mirror framed in a circular molding w/applied spherules & topped by a carved eagle on a rocky perch flanked by leafage, side candle sconces on leafy brackets, leafy-carved base bracket, probably England, ca. 1810, 20" w., 32 1/2" h. **$9,200**

Ornate Rococo Revival Wall Mirror

Rococo Revival wall mirror, gilt gesso, the cartouche-form mirror in a conforming wide molded border w/an outer framework composed of bold ornate pierced leafy scrolls w/a fanned crest, ca. 1900, 16 x 24" **$450**

Aesthetic Movement Overmantel Mirror

Victorian Aesthetic Movement overmantel mirror, walnut & maple, a wide flat top rail centered by a pointed crest w/fanned finial & flanked by a pair of flat stiles at each end w/carved pointed finials above incised leafy bands, the stiles flanking side panels decorated w/Aesthetic floral designs, wide flat bottom rail, in the manner of Isaac Scott, ca. 1870, 60 1/4" l., 31" h. (ILLUS.) **$748**

Victorian Aesthetic Movement substyle cheval mirror, oak, a tall rectangular narrow reeded mirror frame topped by a half-round high pierced crest w/a band of circles & bars set w/two green 'jewels' above an arch of four small spindles, the mirror frame w/bulbous pointed corner finials & swiveling between tall slender columns w/small urn finials, raised on a trestle base w/a wide band of spindles joining the arched legs on casters, ca. 1880-90, 26" w., 73" h. **$2,408**

Victorian Eastlake Pier Mirror

Victorian Eastlake substyle pier mirror, carved walnut, the arched crest w/applied stepped molding over a leafy vine panel flanked by brackets w/turned finials above the slender side rails w/half-round colonettes halfway down above line-incised bands & blocked brackets on a rectangular marble shelf below the tall mirror plate, the base w/a central leaf cluster-carved panel flanked by curved brackets & turned spindles fronting the back panel & resting on a rectangular molded flat base, old finish, ca. 1880 28" w., 92" h. **$1,155**

Fine Renaissance Revival Mirror

Victorian Renaissance Revival overmantel mirror, giltwood, the crestrail carved w/a raised central female mask on an acanthus-topped shield flanked by husk swags, blocked top corners w/palmettes above a raised frieze molding over the large gently arched mirror flanked by block & columnar sides above a molded flat base, w/a marble support shelf, third quarter 19th c., 56" w., 79" h. **$3,335**

Secretaries

Slant Front
Chippendale

The furniture form known as a "secretary" belongs in the large case classification. Secretaries are basically desks with the addition of a cupboard or bookcase-type top section.

Found in almost every furniture style, secretaries are highly functional with detailed interiors full of drawers, pigeonholes, and document storage areas. The French term "secretaire a'abattant" is often used to describe a secretary, especially those with detailed interiors.

Golden Oak Secretary-China Cabinet

Many secretaries are made in two or more parts for ease of construction. Carefully examine both parts of a secretary to make sure that they are both of the same furniture period. A quick way to check this is to look for consistency in design elements and also construction techniques. The type of dovetail used in the top should be identical to the dovetailing found in the base. Drawers should show some signs of wear, as should doors and shelves. Cornices are sometimes a separate piece, being held on with a dowel or fitting well with moldings.

Also see Bookcases and Desks.

French Art Deco Secretary

Art Deco secretary, fruitwood, a rectangular mirrored top w/molded edges above a case w/a heavy rounded molding enclosing an upper wide fall-front panel opening to a fitted interior above a medial band w/an undulating brass strap band above a pair of flat cupboard doors, looped brass pulls, raised on a flared platform base, France, ca. 1940, 17 1/ 2 x 31 1/2", 53" h. **$8,625**

Unusual Arts & Crafts Secretary

Arts & Crafts secretary-bookcase, oak, a rectangular top w/a flaring cornice highlighted by a band of diamonds above a pair of geometrically glazed cupboard doors w/clear panes accented by green slag diamond-shaped panes, raised on incurved sides above the rectangular top over a pair of small drawers flanking the kneehole opening, large half-round cut-outs at the lower sides & arched base cut-out, front stile legs w/through-tenon construction, original finish, probably English, early 20th c., 18 1/2 x 32", 5' 1/4" h. **$2,310**

Fine Chippendale Secretary-Bookcase

Chippendale secretary-bookcase, cherry, two-part construction: the upper section w/a broken-scroll pediment centering a raised spiral-twist finial & flanked by two matching corner finials above a pair of fielded raised panel cupboard doors flanked by reeded pilasters, the interior w/concave shells over three serpentine shelves divided by a cyma-curved vertical board; the lower section w/a hinged slant front opening to a desk interior of valanced compartments & small drawers flanking a prospect door & columns w/a valanced compartment & two small drawers, all above four long graduated cockbeaded drawers on a molded base w/scroll-cut tall bracket feet, old replaced butterfly pulls & key-hole escutcheons, refinished, imperfections, Springfield - Longmeadow, Massachusetts, ca. 1780, 20 3/4 x 38", 7' 2 1/2" h. **$79,500**

Classical Rosewood Secretary

Classical secretary-bookcase, rosewood veneer, two-part construction: the rectangular top w/rounded front corners & a deep coved cornice above a beaded band over a pair of tall Gothic-arch glazed cupboard doors opening to three adjustable shelves over a row of three smaller drawers, the stepped-out lower case w/a hinged narrow fold-down writing surface opening to small satinwood-veneered drawers & valanced compartments over a pair of Gothic arch paneled & beaded cupboard doors on a molded base w/scroll-cut bracket feet, ivory escutcheons & tapered wooden pulls, old refinish, minor losses, New York City, ca. 1840s, 20 5/8 x 44", 94 1/4" h. **$5,175**

Inscribed Federal Secretary

Federal secretary-bookcase, mahogany & mahogany veneer; two-part construction: the top section w/a shallow shaped gallery above a flat molded cornice & two diamond-glazed square doors opening to a small drawer & compartments flanking a square flat central door over a small drawer; the projecting lower section w/a fold-down writing surface above a pair of cockbeaded drawers over two long cockbeaded drawers all w/round brass pulls w/rings, square tapering legs w/inlaid cross-banding, old refinish, imperfections & some restoration, New England, inscribed "22 Geo. L. Deblois September 12th 1810," 20 x 37 1/8", 51 1/2" h. **$2,990**

Federal Secretary-Bookcase

Federal secretary-bookcase, rosewood & birch-inlaid mahogany, two-part construction: the upper section w/a rectangular top w/narrow molded cornice & veneered frieze band over a pair of Gothic arch-glazed cupboard doors opening to two shelves, four short drawers & ten pigeonholes; the stepped-out lower section w/a cross-banded hinged writing flap opening to a tooled leather surface above four cockbeaded long graduated drawers w/oval brasses, band-inlaid apron w/central squared pendant, tall slender French feet, North Shore, Massachusetts, ca. 1810, 20 x 39 3/4", 65" h. **$14,950**

Small George III-Style Secretary

George III-Style secretary-bookcase, mahogany, diminutive size, two-part construction: the upper section w/a broken-arch pediment above a pair of tall narrow geometrically-glazed cupboard doors opening to shelves; the lower section w/a wide hinged slant front opening to a fitted writing compartment above a case w/a pair of small square drawers flanking a longer center drawer over a pair of drawers above two long drawers at the bottom, all w/butterfly pulls & keyhole escutcheons, molded base on scroll-cut bracket feet, England, late 19th c., 19 1/2 x 27", 81" h. **$4,313**

Ornate Late Victorian Secretary

Late Victorian secretary-bookcase, flame cherry & birch, side-by-side style, the left side w/a tall bookcase section w/a serpentine crestrail w/a pierced center opening & carved leafy scrolls above a pair of tall glazed cupboard doors each w/a frosted clear smaller upper pane w/Gothic arch grillwork above long glazed panels w/scroll-trimmed framing, the right side w/a serpentine crestrail over an asymmetrical beveled mirror over a shelf w/a small handkerchief drawer & pierced scroll trim above a hinged slant front decorated w/an ornate scroll-carved panel opening to a fitted interior above a stack of three graduated drawers w/stamped brass pulls, serpentine aprons & bracket feet, old refinish, ca. 1890s, 18 x 48", 5' 6" h. **$2,200**

Queen Anne Secretary

Queen Anne secretary-bookcase, carved & figured maple, two-part construction: the upper section w/a broken swans-neck pediment w/pinwheel terminals surmounted by three turned finials over a pinwheel-carved scrollboard above a pair of tall raised-panel cupboard doors w/tiny knobs & brass keyhole escutcheons opening to an interior fitted w/thirteen pigeonholes; the lower section w/a hinged slant front opening to an interior w/eight valanced pigeonholes & fifteen short drawers, the case w/four long cockbeaded graduated drawers w/butterfly pulls & keyhole escutcheons, molded base on scroll-cut bracket feet, repairs, eastern Connecticut, 1740-60, 18 x 36", 84" h. **$43,125**

Fine Aesthetic Movement Secretary

Victorian Aesthetic Movement secretary, Modern Gothic-style, walnut, the top w/a flat crestrail over a gallery above two panels over a wide double-panel hinged writing surface w/heavy L-shaped brackets opening to a fitted compartment above a long drawer over a pair of recessed paneled doors w/angled metal brackets over two small drawers at the base, molded bottom & blocked side stiles, ca. 1870, 20 1/4 x 36", 63 1/2" h. (ILLUS.) **$2,415**

Victorian Aesthetic Movement secretary-bookcase, walnut, the tall case w/a projecting central section, the top sides w/paneled back rails & spindled supports flanking the taller central section w/a rectangular leaf-carved cornice enclosing a hidden drawer above an open compartment framed at the front by an oval railing enclosing short spindles & backed by a rectangular mirror above a large glazed door w/gilt initials over a fold-down writing surface opening to a fitted interior above a stack of three burl-trimmed drawers, the side sections each w/a low top storage section w/three glass beveled panes above tall glazed cupboard doors w/long vertical half-moon molding w/lattice and vine-carved corner sections, each opening to four shelves, a deep stepped & molded flat base, original finish, ca. 1880s, 20 x 72" , 6' 6" h. **$7,500**

Victorian Country-style Secretary

Victorian country-style secretary-bookcase, walnut, one-piece construction, a rectangular top w/a deep flaring cornice above a pair of tall single-pane glazed doors opening to two shelves above a flat hinged fall-front opening to a writing surface & an interior fitted w/pigeonholes & two small drawers above the lower case w/a pair of paneled cupboard doors, second half 19th c., 19 x 38", 82" h. (ILLUS.) **$660**

Victorian country-style secretary-bookcase, cherry, three-part construction: the upper section w/a deep flaring coved cornice above a pair of tall double-paneled doors w/a short panel over a tall panel & opening to an interior fitted w/two rows of pigeonholes w/two dovetailed drawers, the central projecting section w/a hinged slant front opening to an interior fitted w/a row of four drawers over a row of six pigeonholes, the base w/one dovetailed long drawer above the paneled block-and ring-turned legs w/knob feet, attributed to Kentucky, mid-19th c., old finish, 14 3/4 x 41 1/2" top, 85 1/2" h. (replaced brasses, mid-section nailed to base) **$4,950**

Eastlake Cylinder-front Secretary

Victorian Eastlake substyle cylinder-front secretary-bookcase, walnut & burl walnut, two-part construction: the upper section w/a high stepped crestrail carved w/trefoil finials above blocked panels of trefoils & a central arch over a deep flaring cornice & a saw-tooth-cut frieze band above a pair of tall single-pane glazed doors opening to shelves; the lower section w/a narrow notch-cut band above the burl-paneled cylinder front opening to a fitted interior w/a pull-out writing surface above a case w/a long burl-trimmed line-incised drawer w/stamped brass pulls above two short drawers beside an arched burl-paneled cupboard door, blocked & notched side stiles, deep base band, original hard-ware, refinished, ca. 1885, 26 x 36", 9' h. **$2,500**

Oak Side-by-Side Secretary-Bookcase

Victorian Golden Oak secretary-bookcase, side-by-side style, a high top crest w/scroll-cut sides & a flat crestrail centered by a scroll-carved finial over a narrow half-round shelf on slender spindle supports above an oval beveled mirror above the rectangular top, the left side of the case w/a tall glazed cupboard door w/a scroll-carved top opening to three wood shelves, the right side w/a rectangular mirrored door w/scroll-carved corner above a wide hinged fall-front w/oval carved detail & opening to a fitted interior above a single drawer w/stamped brass pulls over a small paneled cupboard door, scalloped apron & simple stile feet, refinished, ca. 1900, 18 x 40", 5' 8" h. **$1,200**

Victorian Gothic Secretary-Bookcase

Victorian Gothic Revival secretary-bookcase, mahogany & mahogany veneer, two-part construction: the upper section w/a high arched & pierced scroll-carved crestrail w/small turned finials above a plain frieze band over the pair of tall glazed cupboard doors w/quatrefoil & Gothic arch glazing above a pair of thin lower drawers; the lower section w/a stepped-out white marble rectangular top above a single long ogee-front drawer above a pair of Gothic arch-paneled cupboard doors flanked by carved pilasters & ending in heavy block feet, ca. 1840 .... **$3,000**

Victorian Cylinder-front Secretary

Victorian Renaissance Revival cylinder-front secretary-bookcase, walnut & burl walnut, two-part construction: the upper section w/a rectangular top w/deep flaring cornice over frieze band w/narrow raised burl panels & a rondel above a pair of tall arched & glazed cupboard doors opening to shelves; the lower section w/a curved cylinder-front w/burl panels opening to a fitted interior & writing surface above a long slightly projecting drawer w/two raised burl panels above two further long drawers w/burl panels & flanked by carved blocks, plinth base, ca. 1875, 13 3/4 x 43 3/4", 92" h. **$1,870**

Elaborate Rococo Secretary-Bookcase

Victorian Rococo substyle secretary-bookcase, carved mahogany, two-part construction: the upper section w/a high arched scroll-carved cornice centered by a figural bust of Shakespeare above a scroll-carved frieze band above a pair of tall cupboard doors w/ large oval mirror panels framed by ornate carved scrolls over a long narrow scroll-carved drawer; the stepped-out lower section w/a white marble top w/a serpentine front above a long scroll-carved fold-down drawer front revealing the writing surface & interior storage, two cupboard doors below w/large round raised panels surrounding large blossom-form panels & w/carved scrolls in each corner w/further scroll-carving down the side stiles, flat blocked base, original finish, possibly by Mitchells and Rammelsberg of Cincinnati, ca. 1850s, 24 x 55", 8' 9" h. **$8,000**

Sideboards

Mission Oak Sideboard

Sideboards are large case pieces of furniture usually reserved for service in a dining room setting. Their multiple cupboard doors hold accessories, and some are fitted with special racks to hold wine bottles. Drawers are used for the storage of silver and linens. The top of a sideboard often doubled as a buffet or server, resulting in the other common names for sideboards.

Arts & Crafts furniture makers included servers in their dining room suites. Look for original hardware and interesting plate racks as well as mirrors and decorative accents. As with any other furniture of this period, the price is enhanced by knowing the original maker, finding a decal, brand, or label. Original finish also adds to the value.

Classical sideboards show how elaborate this style became as it developed through the years of 1805-1830. The style is typified by

Ornate Victorian Rococo Sideboard

scrolling, but many of these sideboards included carving on their column-type supports, legs, and feet. Tops of many Classical sideboards are either rectangular or rectangular with angular features. Look for additional work surfaces in the form of pull-out slides during this time period.

Sideboards of the Federal period are probably the most sought after by collectors and command the highest prices for this type of furniture. Mahogany and other fine wood was used. Look for decorative inlay on the top, front, and legs. Forms include several variations—bow front, serpentine front, and straight front—with the name derived from the shape of the front. Usually the top corresponds. Legs vary from the tapered square legs to reeded legs, with the tapered square legs being more typical.

Sideboards of the Victorian era illustrate how designers of that time felt bigger was better, and higher was even better. The usage of marble tops, mirrors, carving, and other types of ornamentation were popular. Woods and finishes tend to be dark, adding to the heavy appearance of these sideboards.

Majorelle Art Nouveau Sideboard

Art Nouveau sideboard, carved mahogany, "La Vigne" patt., the superstructure w/a long flat crestrail over a narrow shelf supported by downswept curved supports carved w/grapevines above a paneled back & D-form top over a case w/a pair of paneled drawers above a pair of paneled doors all flanked by boldly carved bands of grapevine & curved side panels, molded serpentine base, Louis Majorelle, France, ca. 1900, 21 3/4 x 102", 72" h. **$14,950**

Arts & Crafts Oak Server

Arts & Crafts server, oak, the superstructure w/a peaked crestrail over a narrow shelf w/an arched apron & tapering supports above a long rectangular mirror, a rectangular top above slightly canted sides enclosing a pair of drawers w/metal pulls above a pair of cupboard doors w/an arched & fanned glazed panel over a plain panel above a single long drawer at the bottom, short stile feet, in the style of the Shop of the Crafters, unsigned, some damage, ca. 1915, 19 1/4 x 42", 37 1/2" h. **$1,265**

Classical Mahogany Server

Bauhaus style sideboard, oak, flat rectangular top on a case w/three flat cupboard doors w/ball-shaped steel pulls, the interior fitted w/four drawers on one side, shelf & drawer on the other side, short square legs, dark brown finish, Germany, ca. 1927, 23 3/4" x 78 3/4", 45" h. (edge nicks, scratches) **$1,150**

Classical server, mahogany & mahogany veneer, a rectangular top above along ogee-molded drawer projecting above a pair of paneled cupboard doors flanked by S-scroll pilasters ending in blocks on C-scroll feet, minor imperfections, Boston, ca. 1825, 18 1/2 x 40", 34" h. (ILLUS.) **$1,725**

Fine Philadelphia Classical Sideboard

Classical sideboard, carved & veneered mahogany, the rectangular top w/molded cornice above a rectangular mirror in a frame flanked by two colonettes w/Corinthian capitals flanked by acanthus- and fruit-carved scrolling volutes over a rectangular case w/two short drawers, each above two tall doors flanked by similar colonettes & capitals centering two long drawers over gadrooning above two shorter paneled doors over a gadrooned band, on foliate-carved & beaded feet on casters, Philadelphia, ca. 1830-40, 23 x 65 1/2", 58" h. **$3,680**

Southern Country-style Sideboard

Country-style sideboard, yellow pine, a rectangular top w/molded edges above a pair of three-panel cupboard doors w/a horizontal panel above two vertical panels, turned wood knobs, molded base raised on baluster- and knob-turned legs, old dark varnished finish, attributed to the Carolinas, early 19th c. **$3,630**

Empire-Style sideboard, gilt-bronze mounted mahogany & mahogany veneer, the super-structure w/a long low arched crest-board w/gilt-bronze winged lion mounts above a narrow rectangular shelf above the long rectangular mirrored back & four

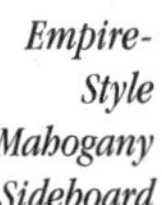

Empire-Style Mahogany Sideboard

marbleized column supports on the rectangular marble top over a band of three narrow drawers w/pierced scrolling gilt-bronze mounts above three cupboard doors w/figural & wreath gilt-bronze mounts & separated by four flat columns w/gilt-bronze capitals & bases, molded base on short heavy turned feet, France, early 20th c., 24 x 77", 72" h. (ILLUS.) **$8,400**

Federal country-style huntboard, walnut, a rectangular top on a deep case w/a pair of deep drawers w/simple turned wood knobs, on slender tall square tapering legs, possibly Tennessee, ca. 1830, 20 x 30", 36" h. **$2,464**

Inlaid Mahogany Federal Server

Federal country-style huntboard, walnut, rectangular top above a deep apron w/a pair of deep beaded-edge dovetailed drawers flanking a narrow matching center drawer, turned wood knobs, on knob-, ring- and rod-turned legs w/ball-and-peg feet, refinished, Southern, first half 19th c., 22 1/4 x 49", 43 3/4" h. (repairs, top replaced) **$2,475**

Federal server, inlaid mahogany, the rectangular top w/a border of lunette inlay above a single long line-inlaid drawer above a pair of central cupboard doors flanked by tall narrow bottle drawers all flanked by reeded stiles & above another border of lunette inlay, a scalloped apron above the square tapering legs, New England, early 19th c., 22 x 38", 41" h. (ILLUS.) .. **$4,025**

Federal Virginia Walnut Sideboard

Federal sideboard, walnut & yellow pine, rectangular top w/molded edges above cockbeaded case w/end drawers, the right drawer visually divided into two drawers & the left w/two working drawers, flanking a central cupboard door w/cockbeading, raised on four tall slender square tapering legs, old oval brass pulls, old refinish, repairs, Virginia, 1790- 1810, 22 x 56", 39" h. (ILLUS.) **$5,520**

Federal sideboard & butler's desk, inlaid mahogany, the elliptical top w/an inlaid edge overhanging a case of veneered cockbeaded drawers & end cupboards outlined w/stringing & having central bone-inlaid keyhole escutcheons as well as a central hinged drawer opening to an interior of small drawers & opening compartments w/a felt-lined writing surface, above a long working drawer & an arched skirt outlined w/patterened inlay, raised on square tapering legs outlined w/stringing & ending in

George III Inlaid Sideboard

cuff inlays, original surface, replaced oval brasses, Boston area, early 19th c., 26 x 62", 41" h. (imperfections) **$14,950**

George III sideboard, satinwood-inlaid mahogany, the rectangular top w/serpentine sides & front above a conforming case fitted w/a central drawer above the shaped skirt & flanked by two doors, all w/crossbanding & line inlay, on square tapering legs ending in spade feet, veneer losses, England, late 18th c., 26 1/2 x 65 1/2", 37" h. (ILLUS.) **$5,462**

Mission-style (Arts & Crafts movement) server, a double-rail plate rack on the rectangular top overhanging a case w/a row of three small drawers above a single long drawer, all w/cast copper oval pulls, square stile legs & rectangular medial shelf, fine new reddish brown finish, branded Gustav Stickley mark, Model No. 819, 20 x 48", 43" h. (small veneer patches on side) **$1,870**

Gustav Stickley Sideboard

Mission-style (Arts & Crafts movement) sideboard, oak, a high closed plate rack above the rectangular top overhanging a case w/a pair of tall flat cupboard doors w/long pointed strap hinges flanking a central stack of four long drawers w/bail pulls, on eight square stile legs, new medium finish, paper label of Gustav Stickley, 25 1/2 x 70", 41" h. **$6,050**

Fine Aesthetic Movement Sideboard

Victorian Aesthetic Movement sideboard, walnut & burl walnut, the superstructure w/a high crowned crest w/a central raised panel w/fan-carved finials over four small leaf-carved panels flanked by line-incised side panels w/fan corner finials above a long narrow shelf supported by front slender turned colonettes & overhanging a large beveled rectangular back mirror flanked by panels w/leaf-carved blocks over the long rectangular marble top over a case w/a row of three burl-paneled drawers over a pair of burl-paneled drawers all projecting above a pair of recessed burl panel doors centered by a carved tall panel of flowers & leaves, carved side rails, molded flat base on casters, ca. 1885 .... **$2,200**

Ornate Baroque-Style Sideboard

Victorian Baroque Revival sideboard, carved oak, two-part construction: the upper section w/a rectangular blocked top fitted w/a high arched & scrolling pierce-carved crest w/a central cartouche flanked by small turned corner finials above the deep flaring cornice w/a scroll-carved frieze band over a pair of tall cupboard doors w/rounded panels w/raised molding enclosing ornately carved game trophies flanked by pierce-carved scrolling brackets & two small shelves above a recessed paneled compartment flanked by ornately carved brackets; the lower section w/a wide rectangular top w/a molded edge over a pair of narrow paneled drawers carved w/grapevines above a pair of paneled cupboard doors w/raised molding enclosing finely carved clusters of fruits, three slender turned columns resting on projecting blocks separate & flank the doors, on compressed bun feet, refinished, Europe, late 19th c., 24 x 60", 9' h. **$5,500**

Ornate Eastlake Carved Sideboard

Victorian Eastlake sideboard, oak, the superstructure w/a pierced & scroll-carved crestrail over a narrow carved band & two raised-panel sections centered by a round beveled mirror flanked by small open shelves w/lattice-carved brackets on slender bobbin-turned spindles all backed by panels w/overall incised leafy vine carving, the rectangular stepped-out top w/molded edge over a pair of line-incised drawers over a long line-incised drawer above a pair of paneled cupboard doors w/a carved band above the recessed panel w/an S-scroll line-incised leafy vine centered by a florette, incised side stiles ending in block feet & a flat plinth base, on casters, ca. 1890, 20 x 43", 68" h. **$920**

Oak Sideboard with Leaded Glass

Victorian Golden Oak sideboard, quarter-sawn oak, the rectangular top w/a wide bowed center section & a long arched crestrail over the conforming case w/small leaded glass windows at the front sides & ends flanking a pair of large bowed & leaded glass doors each centered by a large fleur-de-lis design above a long deep bowed lower drawer all flanked by a short drawer over a deep drawer at each end, gently arched apron, raised on square legs ending in large paw feet on casters, refinished, early 20th c., 20 x 56", 4' h. (ILLUS.) **$1,800**

Victorian Golden Oak sideboard, the tall superstructure w/an arched & scalloped cornice w/rounded scroll-carved corners above an oblong mirror framed by large scrolls & a beaded band above the deeply scalloped open shelf supported by flat uprights & w/bold scroll-carved tops & bases & centered by narrow upright beveled mirrors, also supporting a narrow lower shelf below a large scalloped rectangular beveled mirror, all resting on a rectangular top w/a bowed front above a conforming case w/a pair of drawers over a single long drawer flanked by serpentine side rails above a pair of cupboard doors carved w/a large central oval w/beaded border & flanked by large & small scrolls, narrow rounded base rail flanked by small scrolls, raised on short shaped front feet, refinished, ca. 1900, 20 1/2 x 44", 6' 8" h. **$2,000**

Victorian Renaissance Revival sideboard, carved mahogany, the superstructure w/a long shelf w/rounded ends raised on scroll-carved end brackets & lions head-carved front supports flanking a long low oblong mirror, the rectangular top w/wide rounded front corners above a conforming case, the curved panels carved in bold relief w/pendent fruit clusters, the front case w/three small raised panel drawers w/scroll-carved pulls above three shaped raised paneled cupboard doors each centered by a large carved bunch of pendent game, on a wide molded base, 24 1/2 x 82", 64" h. **$2,300**

Victorian Renaissance Revival sideboard, walnut & burl walnut, the long rectangular white marble top w/molded edges & rounded front corners above a conforming case w/a row of three drawers across the top, two longer drawers w/recessed oval burl panels & cartouche-carved pulls & round keyhole escutcheons flanking a shorter central drawer w/recessed oval burl panel & round keyhole escutcheon all above a pair of large cupboard doors w/recessed large oval burl panels w/raised molding, one w/a relief-carved pair of hanging fish & the other w/a hanging gamebird, a narrow central door w/a plain oval burl panel w/raised molding, on a conforming molded flat plinth base, ca. 1870, 21 1/2 x 59 1/ 2', 36 3/4" h. **$2,310**

Outstanding Victorian Sideboard

Victorian Renaissance Revival sideboard, walnut & burl walnut, the superstructure w/a high arched crestrail centered by a large fanned cartouche-carved crest flanked by carved grapevines above an incised band & burl panels above a molded rail over a scroll-trimmed burl framework enclosing a large arch-topped mirror flanked by carved colonettes & scroll-trimmed small candle shelves over carved block panels, the half-round white marble top w/molded edge & two front projections above a conforming case w/a pair of center drawers w/raised burl panels flanked by rounded side drawers above a pair of flat central cupboard doors w/arched raised panels enclosing burl & large carved grape clusters, matching curved end doors, deep molded base, original finish, ca. 1865, 24 x 74", 8' 2" h. **$8,500**

Ornate Victorian Rococo Sideboard

Victorian Rococo sub-style sideboard, carved walnut, the high superstructure w/an arched & molded crest centered by a shield medallion above a large relief-carved wild game & fish mount, outswept leafy scroll-carved sides over a narrow rectangular shelf above an oval mirror flanked by pierced scroll-carved brackets over the rectangular white marble top w/cut front corners over a conforming case w/a pair of drawers w/recessed oval burl panels w/leaf-carved pulls above a pair of cupboard doors w/large oval burl recessed panels centered by hanging game & fish carved mounts, molded plinth base, ca. 1860-70, 20 3/4 x 54 1/2", 88" h. **$5,170**

Sofas, Love Seats, & Settees

Scarce Child's Windsor Settee

Sofas, settees, love seats, couches, and settles all offered seating. Settees and love seats are the smallest of this group. Sofas and couches are longer and often more generous in the seat. Settles are often considered benches since they lack upholstery. Some settees and sofas were originally part of parlor groups and may include matching arm chairs, rockers, and straight chairs in numerous multiples.

Fine Renaissance Revival Sofa

Early settees and sofas were often included in the inventories of old estates and frequently were listed as part of the bed chamber furnishings. Why? Because during early periods, it was fashionable for the lady of the house to receive some special guests in her bed chamber, and small scale entertaining, such as tea, was often done in these rooms.

Other sofas were listed as part of the hall furnishings, particularly when the hall was large or the person living there was important enough to receive many callers. Sofas are rarely found in inventories before 1820 as the form was not popular until after that time.

Also see Benches.

French Art Deco Daybed

Daybed, Art Deco, rosewood, upright slightly scrolled ends enclosing an upholstered seat above a shaped front apron trimmed w/ormolu, on heavy blocked canted short legs w/ormolu mounts, Jules LeLeu, France, ca. 1935, 85" l., 35" h. (ILLUS.) **$8,050**

Daybed, child's, country-style, painted wood, the shaped back & side panels joining four square tapering posts, old red paint, New England, early 19th c., 22 1/4 x 39 1/2", 32" h. **$1,380**

Classical Country-Style Daybed

Daybed, Classical country-style, walnut, the scroll-carved serpentine crestrail above a solid back panel flanked by outscrolled end arms above the lift-top board seat pulling forward to form a double bed, outswept flat legs w/front center block supports, original finish, New England, ca. 1840-60, 28 x 80", 33" h. (ILLUS.) **$1,100**

Daybed, Federal country-style, painted & decorated, the triple-sectioned back w/turned top rails above a flat center rail & lower rail above rows of short spindles flanked by turned arms over spindles & w/baluster-turned arm supports, a hinged fold-out bed forming the seat w/a deep paneled apron, original yellow ground paint w/brown leaf & berry stencil decoration & striping, New England, early 19th c., replaced seat w/modern textile cover, minor surface imperfections, 18 x 84", 36 1/2" h. (ILLUS. next page) .... **$ 4,025**

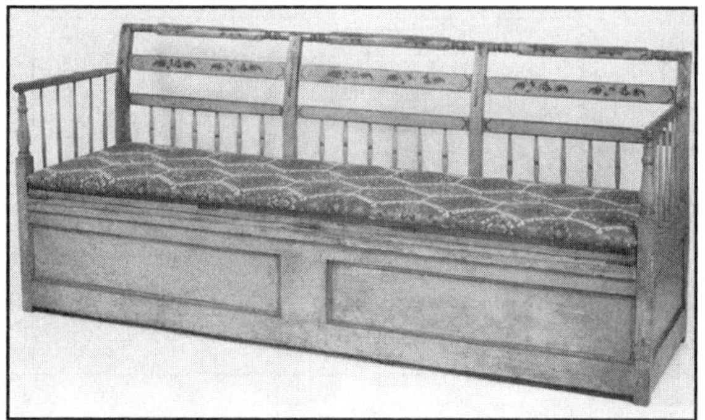

Early Decorated Federal Daybed

Daybed, Mission-style (Arts & Crafts movement), oak, a low slanted back w/angled sides at one end, on a rectangular seat frame w/square post legs, branded Limbert mark, Model No. 850, early 20th c., 30 1/4 x 79 1/4", 24 3/4" h. **$7,050**

Daybed, Mission-style (Arts & Crafts movement), oak, the upright even ends w/heavy square stiles supporting wide flat upper & lower framing six wide slats, wide siderails pinned into end stiles, Gustav Stickley Model No. 220, after 1909, 35 1/2 x 84", 34" h. **$3,450**

Daybed, Modern style, a rectangular seat & back frame in solid maple raised on V-form bent wire legs, fitted w/two checkered pattern rectangular back cushions & a single long seat cushion,

George Nelson Modern Daybed

designed by George Nelson, produced by Herman Miller, ca. 1956, 75" l., 26" h. (ILLUS.) **$1,344**

Daybed, Victorian Renaissance Revival substyle, walnut, the back w/a pair of short scroll-framed hinged end panels pierced w/quatrefoils flanked by matching serpentine end arms w/similar pierced panels all above the deep rectangular rails w/raised panels & center roundels, back panels open allowing the framework to expand to form a full bed, refinished, ca. 1870, 32 x 76" l. closed, 32" h. **$700**

Love seat, Art Deco, ébéne-de-macasar & upholstery, the long narrow arched crestrail above a three-section upholstered back, narrow arm rails w/a raised upholstered central section above a narrow arms, long cushion seat above a narrow gently curved

French Art Deco Love Seat

seatrail, gently swelling arm supports continuing down to form the tapering front legs, tapering rear legs, branded mark of Emile-Jacques Ruhlmann, France, ca. 1925, 63" l. **$43,125**

Love seat, Art Deco, stained beech, a narrow U-form crestrail over the conforming tightly upholstered back & deep upholstered seat flanked by reeded tapering front stile legs, spots on fabric, restorations, France, ca. 1925, 48" l. (ILLUS.) **$2,300**

Fine Classical Méridienne

Méridienne, Classical, carved mahogany, the shaped crestrail carved w/a flowerhead above a conforming padded back, the outscrolled arms w/flowerhead terminals continuing to elaborately-carved flowerheads, the rectangular upholstered seat above conforming seatrail raised on legs carved w/S-scrolls, foliage & fruit & ending in paw feet, American, ca. 1820-30, 88 1/2" l. (ILLUS.) **$5,520**

Méridienne, Victorian Rococo substyle, carved & laminated rosewood, the high arched upholstered curved back at one end enclosed by a scroll-carved border w/a fruit- and flower-carved crest, the oblong serpentine upholstered seat above a conforming floral-carved seatrails, on demi-cabriole legs on casters, John H. Belter, New York, New York, ca. 1850, 42" l., 38" h. **$5,040**

Carved & Painted Belter Méridienne

Méridiennes, carved & painted wood, the low arched & curved upholstered back at one end enclosed by high pierce-carved C-scrolls & ornate floral carvings continuing down the molded end arm, the upholstered oblong serpentine seat on a conforming seatrail w/further ornate leafy scroll & blossom carving, on front demi-cabriole legs ending in scrolls & square rear legs all on casters, John H. Belter, ca. 1855, 25" l., pr. **$14,950**

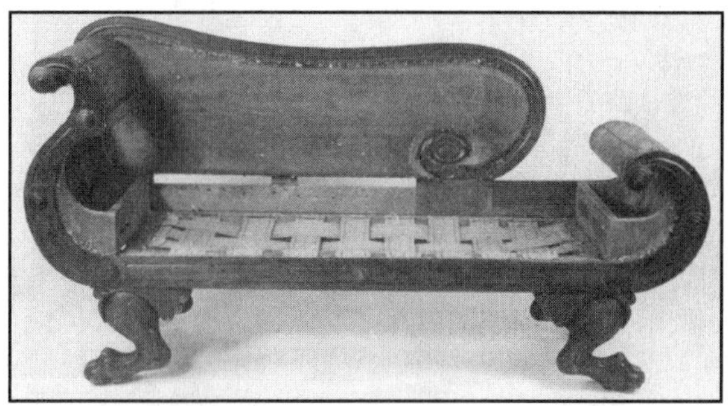

Finely Carved Classical Recamier

Recamier, Classical, mahogany, the molded & shaped back rail continuing to a leaf-carved scroll above the scrolled paneled arms w/concentric ringed bosses, above a paneled seatrail & carved paw feet on casters, Boston, old finish, ca. 1825, 65 1/8" l. (ILLUS.) **$8,625**

Recamier, Classical, brass-mounted carved mahogany & mahogany veneer, of box form, an upright squared end w/a heavy rounded crestrail along the arm & long back & terminating at each end w/a leaf-carved scroll, the closed upholstered arm & low back panel opposite the out-scrolled end w/cornucopia-carved support, long upholstered seat on a flat seatrail, the closed arm w/a columnar arm support w/brass-mounted capital & base, on heavy short legs w/a carved acanthus leaf cluster over a bulbous reeded knob foot, New York, ca. 1815, 34 x 86", 16" h. **$8,400**

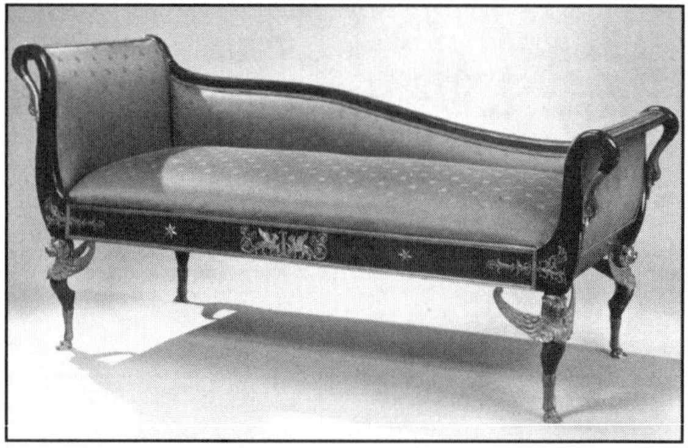

Empire-Style Recamier

Recamier, Empire-Style, gilt-bronze mounted mahogany, the low undulating back continuing to rolled arms terminating in carved swans heads, above a simple rectangular upholstered seat w/straight seatrail mounted w/gilt-bronze winged lions, stars & scrolls, raised on figural legs headed by gilt winged lion heads & ending in paw feet, France, late 19th c., 72 1/2" l. (ILLUS.) **$4,888**

Recamier, Federal, mahogany, a narrow reeded downward curving crestrail above the upholstered back & joining a high & low scrolled end arm w/reeded scrolled framing continuing down to

English Regency Inlaid Recamier

the reeded seatrail, on reeded sabre legs ending in brass paw feet w/casters, probably Boston, early 19th c., 76" l. **$7,475**

Recamier, Regency, brass-inlaid beechwood, a long low upholstered back w/serpentine molded crestrail ending in an inlaid brass pinwheel, the curved upholstered end arm w/a carved arm support, the long oblong seat w/a wide reeded seatrail decorated w/inlaid scrolling brass plaques above the heavy carved acanthus leaf legs on reeded knob feet on casters, long seat cushion & bolster pillow, England, second quarter 19th c., 76" l. (ILLUS.) **$4,600**

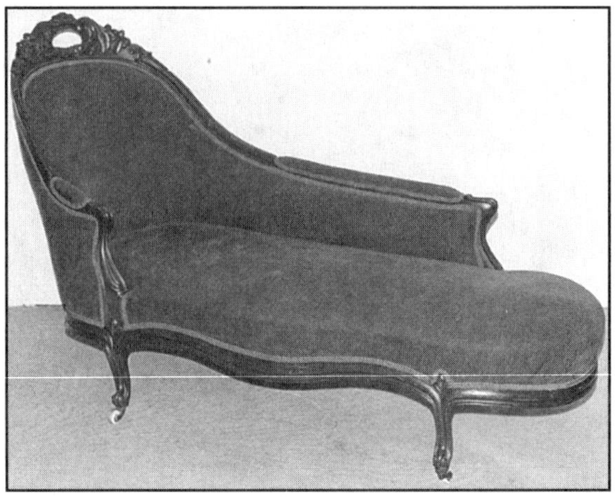

Victorian Rococo Recamier

Recamier, Victorian Rococo substyle, walnut, the high arched & rounded back w/a scroll-carved crestrail w/a pierced hand grip continuing down to form a short padded & closed side arm & a long low padded back rail, long oval upholstered seat on a finger-carved serpentine seatrail, raised on demi-cabriole legs w/porcelain casters, early reupholstery, ca. 1860, 24 x 68", 36" h. (ILLUS.) **$950**

Recamiers, Federal-Style, parcel-gilt & ebonized wood, the outscrolled open back rest formed w/turned & paneled slats

Federal-Style Decorated Recamier

above a long shaped arm over the narrow rectangular caned seat on slender knob- and ring-turned splayed legs joined by turned stretchers, decorated overall w/Classical designs in gold on black, some wear, ca. 1900, 76" l., pr. (ILLUS.) **$2,875**

Settee, Chippendale-Style, mahogany, the delicately carved slender triple-arch crestrail above delicate scroll- and swag-carved pierced splats, slender curved open-end arms on incurved arm supports, upholstered spring seat w/a thin serpentine seatrail, slender carved cabriole front legs & square canted rear legs, old finish, early 20th c., 42" l. **$770**

Classic Austrian Bentwood Settee

Settee, bentwood, beechwood, the shaped rectangular back composed of sinuous open curves & swirls above the long oval caned seat flanked by curled bentwood arms, on slender turned & gently curved legs joined by a high oval bentwood stretcher, designed by Joseph Hoffmann, fragmentary maker's paper label, Austria, ca. 1905, wear, 45" l. **$3,450**

Finely Carved Classical Settee

Settee, Classical, carved mahogany, the upholstered double-shield-form back centered by a carved spread-winged eagle above a veneer panel, scrolled back stiles above the deep semi-overupholstered seat on a bolection-molded plinth & eagle-carved legs ending in paw feet, formerly fitted w/casters, probably New York City, ca. 1825, 72" l. (ILLUS.) **$6,325**

Settee, Edwardian, painted satinwood, the rectangular back frame w/a raised, painted central crest panel above a long rectangular caned panel flanked by pierced panels w/forked splats centered by a decorated oval medallion, a pierced lattice band along the bottom of the back, slender open downswept arms on molded supports above the caned seat w/a loose button cushion,

Federal Revival Triple-back Settee

raised on square tapering legs ending in spade feet, painted w/flowers & classical designs, England, ca. 1900 (repairs, chips). **$3,120**

Settee, Federal Revival style, mahogany, triple-back form, the back composed of three oval sections enclosed pierced vase-form splats topped w/a carved urn & swags, shaped slender open arms on incurved arm supports above the wide overupholstered seat, raised on square tapering legs joined by a long H-stretcher, late 19th c., reupholstered in the 1920s, original finish, 22 x 58", 40" h. (ILLUS.) **$1,600**

Scandinavian-American Settee

Settee, Scandinavian-American country-style, painted pine, mortise & tenon construction, the wide scallop-cut crestrail above three rectangular panels w/slender spindles, high outscrolled end arms w/turned top rails over curved lower rails, the long rectangular hinged seat above a deep well, short square stile legs, original grey paint, ca. 1870, 21 x 80", 36" h. (ILLUS.) **$1,200**

Settee, Louis XVI-Style, hardwood, long oval back w/gadroon-carved frame around central caning, open padded end arms w/carved incurved arm supports above the caned seat w/a fitted

Simple Victorian Rococo Settee

cushion, gadroon-carved seatrail, turned reeded legs w/peg feet, early 20th c., 46 1/2" l. **$880**

Settee, Victorian Rococo substyle, walnut, the serpentine crestrail w/finger-carving curved down to form closed padded arms & curved arm supports, vertically tufted back, upholstered spring seat, serpentine finger-molded seatrail between demi-cabriole front legs on casters, light blue velvet upholstery, ca. 1860, repairs, 62 1/4" l. (ILLUS.) **$358**

Settee, William & Mary-Style, oak, the high double-arched upholstered back flanked by shaped upholstered wings above the rolled upholstered arms, long cushion seat above the scalloped

Windsor Birdcage Style Settee

upholstered seatrail, raised on onion- and block-turned front legs & square canted rear legs joined by two sets of flattened double-arched stretchers, old worn finish, early 20th c., Europe, 60" l. **$935**

Settee, Windsor birdcage style, maple & pine, a triple-section back w/a pair of upper crestrails in each section centered by a rectangular tablet & two tiny spindles above the lower back composed of numerous bamboo-turned spindles & bamboo-turned stiles, the bamboo-turned open arms w/two short spindles & a canted arm support above the long rectangular plank seat raised on eight bamboo-turned canted legs joined by bamboo-turned stretchers, old refinish, imperfections, New England, ca. 1810, 78" l., 33" h. (ILLUS.) **$3,220**

Gustav Stickley Signed Settee

Settee, Mission-style (Arts & Crafts movement), oak, a wide V-back top rail above twelve vertical slats between the square stiles, flat shaped arms on square front stile legs w/corbels under the arms, recovered leather seat, wide flat front & rear stretchers & narrow double side stretchers, large red decal mark of Gustav Stickley, Model No.212, 24 x 48", 36" h. **$3,300**

Early High-Back Painted Settle

Settle, painted pine, the high back constructed of beaded horizontal boards above the seat w/a hinged top over the deep straight front & cut-out feet, tall shaped arms formed by end boards, old red varnish over earlier blue paint, New England, early 19th c., imperfections, 16 x 42", 49" h. **$18,400**

Unusual Gustav Stickley Settle

Settle, Mission-style (Arts & Crafts movement), oak, the tall solid paneled back w/rounded side wings w/oval cut-out continuing to form low side arms flanking the wide lift-seat w/a deep apron, cut-out low feet, through-tenon construction, recoated original fin-ish, some distress to the sides, red decal mark of Gustav Stickley, Model No. 224, 22 x 48", 45" h. **$4,400**

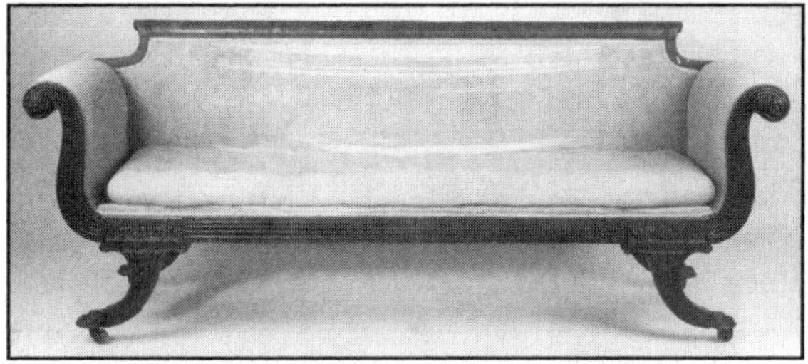

Duncan Phyfe-Attributed Sofa

Sofa, Baroque-Style, carved walnut, the simple rectangular back w/an elaborate mounted crest in the form of a grotesque mask surrounded by foliate scrolls, flanked by winged female figures, Europe, late 19th c., 85" l. **$3,737**

Sofa, Chippendale-Style, mahogany, camel-back design w/a serpentine upholstered crestrail above a canted back over outward scrolling arms above an overupholstered rectangular seat, on Marlborough legs joined by H-stretchers, 20th c., 30 x 90", 38" h. **$2,760**

Sofa, Classical, carved mahogany, the long narrow rolled single paneled crestrail above out-scrolled arms w/reeded arm supports punctuated w/carved rosettes, upholstered back, arms & cushion seat, reeded seatrail w/flanking panels of foliate & leaf carving above reeded sabre legs on brass paw feet on casters, old surface, minor imperfections, attributed to the workship of Duncan Phyfe, New York City, 1815-25, 85" l. (ILLUS.) **$4,600**

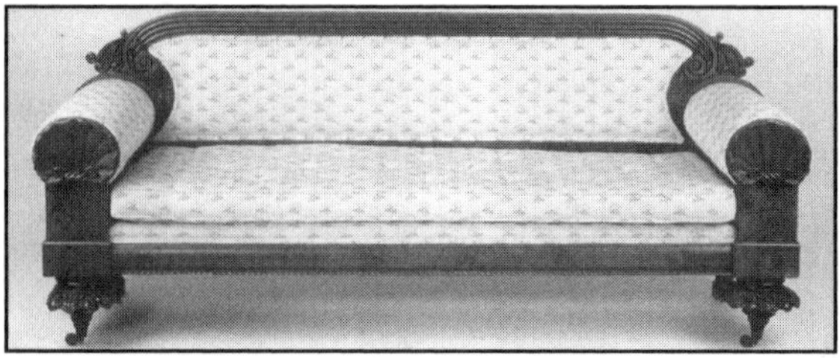

Attractive Classical Sofa

Sofa, Classical, carved & veneered mahogany, a gently arched reeded crestrail w/scroll-carved terminals over the upholstered back & flanked by rolled arms w/applied carved frontal shells over the cushion seat & seatrail w/gadrooning on front egg-and-dart-carved feet on casters w/ring-turned rear feet, Baltimore or Philadelphia, ca. 1825-35, imperfections, 84" l. (ILLUS.) **$690**

Sofa, Classical, mahogany & mahogany veneer, the long straight round crestrail ending in leaf-carved downturned scroll ends above the long low upholstered back flanked by outswept S-scroll upholstered arms w/leaf- and scroll-carved arm supports, a long straight rounded seatrail over the paw feet, original finish, old but not original upholstery, ca. 1830, 76" l., 36" h. **$2,400**

Sofa, Classical, mahogany & mahogany veneer, the raised crestrail w/rope-carved top & incurved ends above the upholstered back flanked by out-scrolling arms w/floral & cornucopia-carved arm supports continuing to carved panels & a flat molded seatrail raised on figural dolphin-carved front legs & turned back legs, refinished, reupholstered, first quarter 19th c., 107" l. .. **$3,850**

Massachusetts Federal Sofa

Sofa, Danish Modern style, teak, a long rectangular tack back frame joined to the seat by two steel rods, slanted teak armrests similarly joined to seat, tapered legs, repeating fan design on the salmon-colored upholstered back, seat & arm cushions, Hans Wegner, Denmark, ca. 1955, 82" l., 30 1/4" h. **$575**

Sofa, Federal, mahogany & mahogany veneer, the narrow flat reeded crestrail above an upholstered back & downswept arm rails over closed arms & baluster-turned arm supports, a long cushion seat over the curved seatrail on four turned & tapering front legs on brass casters & four square tapering rear legs on casters, old refinish, imperfections, some height loss, Boston or North Shore, Massachusetts, ca. 1815-20, 13 x 76", 34 1/8" h. (ILLUS.) **$7,475**

Louis XV-Style Upholstered Sofa

Sofa, Louis XV-Style, carved mahogany, triple-back style, the oblong upholstered center medallion enclosed by narrow pierced-carved molding continuing around the arched serpentined upholstered side panels, serpentine arm rails continuing to incurved front arm support, three-cushion seat, serpentine apron w/a scroll-carved serpentine seatrail, on serpentine front legs ending in scroll feet, original finish & upholstery, ca. 1920s, 76" l., 36" h. (ILLUS.) **$800**

Sofa, Mission-style (Arts & Crafts movement), oak, a single wide back rail & even end arms w/five slats at each end flanking the

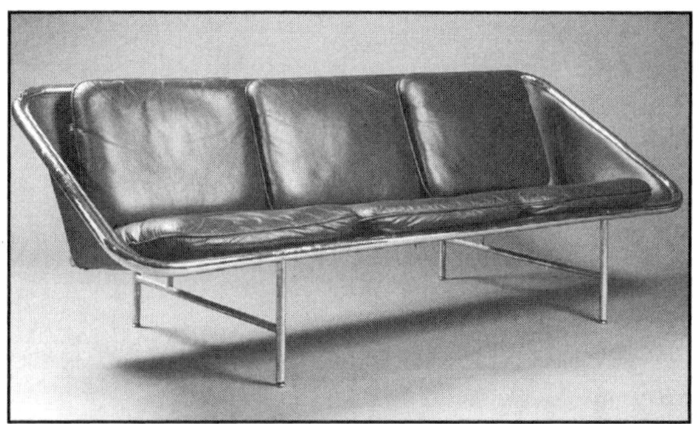

George Nelson "Sling" Sofa

original leather-covered drop-in spring seat w/some tears, original light finish, paper label & decal of Gustav Stickley, Model No. 225, 31 x 78", 29" h. **$4,950**

Sofa, Modern style "Sling" style, leather & chrome, a heavy gauge chrome tube steel framework supporting three leather back & seat cushions, on slender tubular steel legs, designed by George Nelson, manfactured by Herman Miller, ca. 1964, 31 1/2 x 86", 28 7/ 8" h. (ILLUS.) **$4,600**

Sofa, Queen Anne-Style, walnut, rectangular-framed upholstered back over outscrolled arms, three loose cushions in seat, raised on cabriole front legs ending in pad feet, floral upholstery, England, early-20th c., 76 1/2" l., 39" h. **$1,840**

Victorian Baroque Revival Sofa

Sofa, Victorian Baroque Revival style, carved mahogany, a wide flat crestrail ornately carved w/leafy scrolls flanking a central cartouche joining wide scroll-carved stiles above the upholstered back & padded rounded arms over upholstered sides & blocked columnar scroll-carved arm supports flanking the long upholstered seat, a gadroon-carved flat seatrail & heavy block front feet, ca. 1890-1900. (ILLUS.) **$2,500**

Sofa, Victorian Egyptian Revival substyle, ebonized & brass-mounted, the gently arched upholstered crest flanked by rails w/leaf-and-berry carving further flanked by brass-mounted lions' heads w/open jaws above an upholstered back over tufted arms above scrolled supports fronted by brass-mounted Egyptian busts over a partially overupholstered triple-lobed seatrail centered by a

Triple-back Victorian Rococo Sofa

brass-mounted lion's head, on sabre legs w/brass-mounted hoof feet, the mounts stamped "PS," attributed to Pottier & Stymus, New York City, ca. 1880, 72" l. **$9,200**

Sofa, Victorian Rococo substyle, walnut, triple-back style w/a large oval upholstered central panel flanked by oval upholstered panels each w/finger-carved frames & floral- and leaf-carved crests, raised above a long upholstered seat flanked by padded open arms on curved arm supports, serpentine molded & carved seatrail joined to demi-cabriole legs on casters, canted back legs w/casters, ca. 1860. (ILLUS.) **$1,680**

Victorian Renaissance Revival Rosewood Sofa

Sofas, Victorian Renaissance Revival substyle, carved rosewood, a long narrow gently arched crestrail centered by a carved cartouche w/shell & scrolls flanked by molded stiles headed by scroll-carved finials on floral-incised plinths w/carved drapery above the tufted upholstered back over padded arms on downswept arm supports above the long tufted upholstered seat w/a bowed seatrail trimmed w/raised banding centering an oval reserve above a shaped pendant, on tapering turned legs on casters, probably New York City, ca. 1875, 68 1/4" l., 44" h., pr. **$5,750**

Unusual Late Victorian Tete-a-Tete

Tete-a-tete, Golden Oak style, a pair of wide balloon-form opposing backs tapering to a pierced & leafy scroll-cut section above a shaped rectangular seat, backs joined by a centralrail over spindles, curved end arms over turned spindles & arm supports, knob-turned edges joined by knob-turned stretchers, ca. 1900. .... **$1,400**

Primitive Painted Wagon Seat

Wagon seat, painted wood, primitive country-style, a narrow square crestrail & matching lower rail flanked by turned tapering back leg stiles & forming a two-section back w/seven slender turned spindles in each section, open turned arms above the two-part early splint seat above six heavy turned legs, original red paint, New England, mid-19th c., imperfections, 34 1/4" l., 17" h. **$460**

Stands

Chippendale Washstand

Most furniture styles include some kind of specialized stand. Often these are named to represent their function. Stands are found in almost all kinds of wood and some interesting uses of metal, leather, and marble.

Book stands were popular in several different furniture periods. The idea was that an open book could be placed on the stand for reading. Many times heavy reference books, such as dictionaries, were placed on this kind of stand.

Candlestands were designed to hold a candle or lamp. Their high cabriole legs allowed them to be placed close to chairs or tables. Some candlestands were made with a tilting mechanism so that the top could be turned to facilitate placing the stand close to a wall when not it use. The term "tilt-top" is the common name for this type of mechanism. Reproductions of this popular form abound. Look for signs of wear, age to the wood, and original period finishes.

The Arts & Crafts period designers created the drink stand, which is a small stand with a top designed to hold a glass or small

Federal Cherry Candlestand

decanter. The shelf below could hold other bar-ware type articles.

Magazine stands were popular with English designers and are often called Canterburys. It was the Arts & Crafts period of American furniture making that really embraced this style of stand.

Music has played an important part in the lives of people for generations. It was once quite stylish to give musicals in the home, and to do this properly, an elegant music stand was needed to complement the rest of the decor of the music room.

Nightstands are stands found in bedrooms. Just as we use nightstands today, these stands held clocks, lamps, and whatever else was needed close at hand during the night. The other function for nightstands is found in a hallway or at the top of stairs, and then their primary function was to hold a candle or lamp. Because the usage is so general, it is often difficult to definitely identify a stand as a nightstand.

Plant stands were important decorative accessories in several furniture styles. Look for plant stands to have a plain top over a more ornate pedestal. They usually are supported by sturdy legs as a base. Always look for signs of water damage and dents or chips as this type of stand was easily tipped over.

Shaving stands are clever inventions designed to hold the implements one needed for daily grooming tasks, including shaving. A mirror is an important part of this type of stand. Many stands were made to tilt to suit the comfort of the user.

Smoking stands were created to hold a smoker's accessories and usually contained an ashtray. Some had compartments for tobacco or pipes and matches. Look for signs of wear and usage when purchasing a vintage smoking stand. When the stand includes doors and more elaborate fittings, they are generally called a smoking cabinet.

Washstands are a larger stand found in a bedroom. The form was designed to hold a wash bowl, pitcher, and the accompanying accessories, such as a soap dish, toothbrush holder, smaller pitcher, shaving mug, etc. A lower shelf might hold a chamber pot or large slop jar. Before the days of indoor plumbing, washstands were a necessity. Some include small vertical pieces on the back, known as backsplashes. Very elaborate washstands may have cutouts for the individual pieces and even towel bars on the sides. As the age of machine-made furniture came into being, many washstands were made to be part of the matching pieces in a bedroom suite. Earlier furniture styles had more of a simplistic design.

Stickley Bros. Mission Bookstand

Bookstand, Mission-style (Arts & Crafts movement), oak, rectangular top w/three-quarters gallery above three open shelves flanked by three narrow side slats, square stile legs, Stickley Bros., Grand Rapids, Michigan, Model No. 4708, refinished, wear, medium brown finish, 12 x 26 3/4", 38 1/2" h. **$1,035**

Fine Chippendale Candlestand

Candlestand, Chippendale, carved & figured mahogany & walnut, the round top tilting above a slender flaring standard & urn-form support on a tripod base w/cabriole legs ending in claw-and-ball feet, chips to feet, New York City, ca. 1770, 20 1/2" d., 27 1/2" h. **$5,175**

Classical Country Candlestand

Candlestand, Classical country-style, tiger stripe maple, a rectangular top w/canted corners on a baluster-, urn- and ring-turned pedestal on a tripod base w/flat outswept S-scroll legs, old finish, New England, ca. 1825, 16 3/4 x 21 3/4", 28 1/2" h. **$1,390**

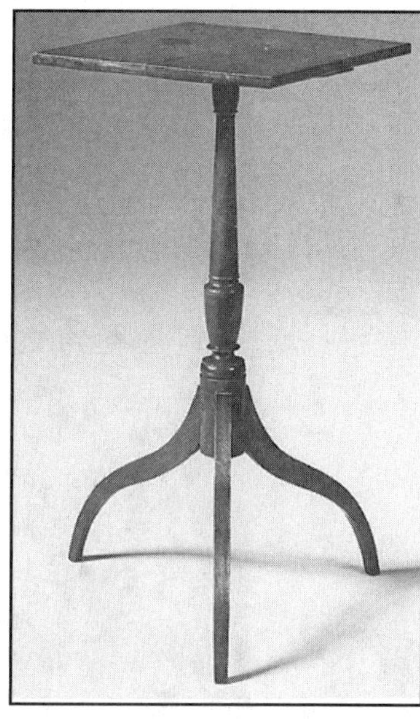

Federal Country-style Candlestand

Candlestand, Federal country-style, birch, the square top above a slender slightly flaring standard on an urn-form support on a tripod base w/spider legs, top stained, slightly warped, northern New England, ca. 1800, 14 1/2 x 15 1/4", 28 1/4" h. ... **$1,150**

Queen Anne Candlestand

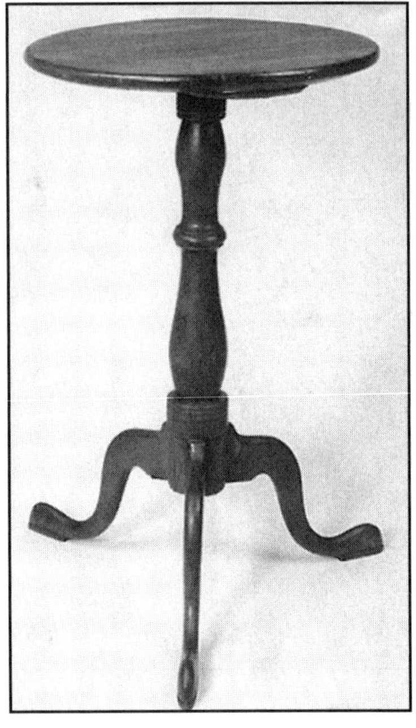

Candlestand, Queen Anne, cherry, the round top on a baluster- and ring-turned standard on a tripod base w/flattened cabriole legs ending in arris pad feet on platforms, old refinish, possibly Vermont, 18th c., 15 1/4" d., 25 3/4" h. **$1,035**

Early Windsor Candlestand

Candlestand, Windsor, a central candlearm w/a socket at each end adjusting on a screw-turned central post above a round dished platform on a simple turned post on a small thick disk on three tall canted turned legs, old dark finish, candle cups later, New Hampshire, late 18th c., 13" d., 36" h. **$1,840**

Rare Mission Oak Drink Stand

Drink stand, Mission-style (Arts & Crafts movement), oak, a round copper-clad top over-hanging a conforming apron on four heavy square canted legs joined by wide cross stretchers, L. & J.G. Stickley (ILLUS.) **$17,680**

Drink stand, Mission-style (Arts & Crafts movement), oak, a round top above cross braces on four tall square legs joined by lower cross stretchers & a small round shelf, new finish on top, original finish on the base, "Handcraft" label of L. & J.G. Stickley, 18" d., 29" h. **$990**

Onyx & Brass Victorian Fern Stand

Fern stand, late Victorian, brass & onyx, an onyx diamond-form top shelf set in a pierced brass frame raised on four spiral-twist supports w/onyx disk finials above a matching lower onyx shelf raised on slender outswept tapering legs w/scroll tips on flat disks, original finish, ca. 1890, 16 x 20", 32" h. **$450**

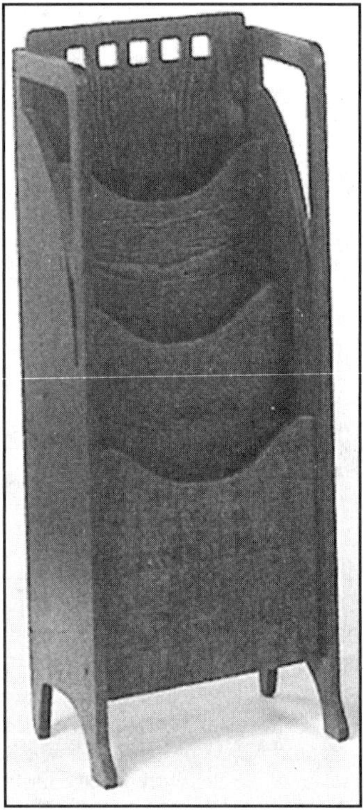

Arts & Crafts Magazine Stand

Magazine stand, Arts & Crafts style, oak, narrow upright form w/three vertical slots under a back containing five small square cut-outs w/arched & cut-out sides, recent finish, unsigned Lakeside Craftshop, early 20th c., 10 x 14", 38" h. **$1,210**

Classical Mahogany Nightstand

Nightstand, Classical, carved mahogany & mahogany veneer, the rectangular top w/gadrooned edges above a single long curved-front drawer w/pressed glass pulls flanked by leaf-carved panels & above a gadrooned apron band, raised on ring- and knob-turned leaf-carved supports over a medial shelf w/shaped front, on carved blocks over short turned legs w/knob feet, probably Philadelphia, ca. 1825, minor imperfections, refinished, 17 x 25", 29" h. **$978**

Renaissance Revival Nightstand

Nightstand, Victorian Renaissance Revival substyle, walnut & burl walnut, the rectangular white marble top w/molded edges above a case w/rounded front corners flanking a single drawer w/burl panels flanking a roundel w/wooden knob, a medial molding above the conforming lower case w/a paneled door centered by a raised burl panel w/a carved floral cluster & wooden knob, deep molded base on rounded thin block feet, refinished, ca. 1875, 16 x 18", 30" h. **$900**

Fine French Art Nouveau Nightstand

Nightstands, Art Nouveau, carved mahogany & rosewood, an arched & paneled crestboard w/pierced loops & floral-carved crest above the brown marble-inset top above a small drawer raised on molded & forked open brackets continuing to the slender square molded front supports joined by a medial shelf, solid back panels above the base shelf on a scroll-carved apron on short curved feet, possibly by Louis Majorelle, France, one w/a lower door, ca. 1900, 11 1/2 x 15", 41" h., pr. (ILLUS. of one) **$8,050**

Louis XV-Style Inlaid Nightstands

Nightstands, Louis XV-Style, inlaid mahogany, the rectangular top w/a serpentine front & low carved gallery above a deep case w/two drawers w/small ring pulls & veneered in a continuous design form a central oval w/flowers within a larger shield-form inlaid panel, side stiles w/carved flowers & ribbon-tied reeds above the simple cabriole legs w/scroll feet flanking the deep serpentine apron, original finish, early 20th c., 15 x 20", 28" h., pr. **$900**

Nightstands, Modern style, enamel-mounted limed oak, a flat rectangular top above a case w/two deep blocked drawers mounted w/green enameled pulls, raised on short round taper-

Modern Style Nightstand

ing feet, labeled Karpen - Guaranteed - Furniture, ca. 1950, finish distressed, 18 x 21", 23 1/2" h., pr. (ILLUS. of one) **$805**

Pedestal stands, Victorian Neoclassical style, giltwood, round marble-inset top w/a molded edge above a beaded apron supported on four slender incurved legs topped w/scrolled medallions joined by open swags surrounding a central reeded post, the legs joined by a medial ring stretcher & ending in hoof feet, on a round molded platform base, ca. 1870, 15" d., 42" pr. **$3,500**

Golden Oak Turned Plant Stand

Plant stand, Golden Oak, a bulbous baluster-turned pedestal supporting a stepped round top, on a round platform base raised on four paw-and-bun feet, refinished, ca. 1900, 14" d., 32" h. **$550**

Plant stand, painted pine, three graduated demi-lune tiers on turned supports over a base of turned posts on arched feet joined by turned stretchers, old green paint, New England, late 19th c., 18 1/2" x 37 3/4", 36" h. **$748**

Victorian Rococo Shaving Stand

Reading stand w/canterbury, Federal, mahogany, the rectangular lattice stand above a baluster- and ring-turned post on a rectangular canterbury base w/pairs of slender turned spindles forming six slots, on casters, labeled "Blanchard and Parson No. 294 North Market Street, Albany," Albany, New York, early 19th c., 14 x 22 1/4", 47 1/2" h. **$3,105**

Shaving stand, Victorian Rococo substyle, walnut, the rectangular top set w/a small oval-framed mirror w/scroll-carved crest swiveling between scroll- and leaf-carved uprights, the shallow case w/two narrow drawers w/line-incised decoration & small knobs & turned corner drops, raised on a slender reeded columnar pedestal on a tripod base w/flared serpentine legs set w/tiny urn finials, on small brass casters, ca. 1860, 16" w., 5' 8" h. (ILLUS.) **$1,650**

Mission Oak Smoker's Stand

Smoking stand, Mission-style (Arts & Crafts movement), oak, a rectangular top overhanging a case w/a small drawer above a tall paneled door, both w/hammered copper pulls, slightly arched aprons, short square stile feet, medium brown finish, red decal mark of L. & J. G. Stickley, Model No. 26, ca. 1907, wear, 15 x 20", 29 1/4" h. **$4,888**

Tiger Stripe & Bird's-eye Maple Washstand

Washstand, Classical country-style, tiger stripe & bird's-eye maple, the high scrolled backsplash & scrolled lower sides on the rectangular top over a single long drawer w/a simple turned wood knob raised on rod- and ring-turned supports to the rectangular medial shelf w/block corners on ring-turned short legs w/knob feet, refinished, imperfections, probably Pennsylvania, ca. 1825, 17 x 21 3/4", 29" h. **$1,150**

Massachusetts Classical Washstand

Washstand, Classical, mahogany & mahogany veneer, the top w/a high three-quarters gallery w/a raised scroll-cut center crest above the rectangular bow-fronted top w/a large bowl cut-out, the bowed apron flanked by two small square drawers, the incurved sides above a lower shelf over a single drawer w/replaced brass pulls, raised on spiral-turned legs w/knob feet, refinished, probably North Shore, Massachusetts, ca. 1825, minor imperfections, 14 1/2 x 20 1/2", 51 1/4" h. **$1,150**

Fine Portsmouth Area Washstand

Washstand, Federal, corner-style, inlaid mahogany, the pointed arch & shaped splash-board centered by a quarter-round shelf above a round-fronted top w/a pierced basin hole, the edge w/square string inlay, raised on three square supports continuing to an open shelf over a satinwood veneered apron centered by a small drawer, string inlay on the supports & the three outswept lower legs joined by three slender tapering stretchers centered by an inlaid patera, patterned inlay trim, old finish, minor imperfections, Portsmouth, New Hampshire area, ca. 1800, 16 1/2 x 23", 41" h. **$5,750**

Rare Curly Maple Federal Washstand

Washstand, Federal country-style, curly maple, a high shaped backsplash flanked by stepped sides on the rectangular top w/a large central bowl cut-out, raised on ring- and baluster-turned supports above a medial shelf over a single drawer w/early pressed glass knob, on baluster- and ring-turned legs, refinished, early 19th c., 17 x 20", 33" h. (ILLUS.) **$3,410**

Washstand, Federal "tambour-front" style, mahogany, the top arched & reeded sides centering a retracting tambour top on paneled dies centering a drawer over a cupboard door on turned & reeded legs w/baluster-turned legs on casters, appears to

Federal Tambour-front Washstand

retain original cast-brass hardware, losses to veneer, missing fitted interior, New York City, ca. 1810, 20" sq., 36 1/2" h. (ILLUS.) **$1,495**

Washstand, Modern style, blue-painted wood, the rectangular superstructure w/graduated planes, a high rectangular back-splash w/clipped corners & ceramic tile insets decorated w/a royal blue Secessionist design, side drawer, towel rack & an open bay above a small cabinet door, together w/a matching ceramic water pitcher, wash bowl & cov. bucket, each w/matching Secessionist design, Austria, early 20th c., stand 24 1/8 x 26", 44" h., the set **$2,233**

Painted Victorian Cottage Washstand

Washstand, Victorian cottage-style, painted & decorated pine, the tall splashback w/beveled corners fitted w/two small shelves w/brackets above the rectangular top over a case w/a long drawer w/two narrow oblong brass pulls over a pair of cupboard doors on a molded base, original painted decoration of outlined panels & stylized florals w/brown & grey flowers, black striping, etc., wear, some edge damage, ca. 1880, 14 3/4 x 29 1/4", 35 1/2" h. **$248**

Decorated Victorian Washstand

Washstand, Victorian country-style, painted & decorated pine, a rectangular hinged top w/molded edges opening to a deep well above a small working drawer beside a faux drawer over a heavy mid-molding & a lower rectangular door, serpentine apron, grain-painted ground w/painted panels simulating bird's-eye maple & dark wood, fine finish, second half 19th c., 18 x 29", 31" h. **$303**

Signed Victorian Walnut Washstand

Washstand, Victorian Renaissance Revival substyle, walnut & burl walnut, the rectangular white marble top w/a serpentine splashback & molded edges, on a case w/a single drawer w/raised burl panels & T-form drop pulls flanked by ring-turned quarter-round corners above blocked & carved edges flanking the single door w/an arched central panel w/a raised fruit-carved central reserve & shaped burl panels at the top corners, deep molded base w/rounded corners, stenciled label in drawer for Mitchell & Rammelsberg Co., Cincinnati, Ohio, refinished, ca. 1875, 16 x 20", 36" h. **$1,900**

Classcial Country Two-drawer Stand

Classical country-style two-drawer stand, bird's-eye maple, tiger stripe maple & cherry, the nearly square thick top slightly overhanging the deep apron w/two drawers each w/two large turned wood pulls, raised on baluster-, rod- and ring-turned legs ending in knob feet, old refinish, imperfections, possibly Pennsylvania, ca. 1825, 19 x 21 1/2", 29" h. **$1,610**

Federal Mahogany One-drawer Stand

Federal one-drawer stand, mahogany, a square top overhanging an apron w/a single drawer above ring-turned & reeded legs ending in peg feet in brass casters, refinished, Massachusetts, ca. 1810-15, minor restoration, 19 x 19 1/4", 27 1/2" h. (ILLUS.) **$1,840**

Federal two-drawer stand, painted birch & bird's-eye maple, the rectangular top overhanging a deep apron w/two cock-beaded graduated drawers w/bird's-eye maple fronts, the borders stained to imitate inlay, on slender square tapering legs, simple bail pulls & oval keyhole escutcheon appear to be original, New England, ca. 1810, 13 1/2" x 17 1/8", 28 3/4" h. (minor imperfections) **$2,990**

Gustav Stickley One-drawer Stand

Magazine stand, Victorian Eastlake substyle, walnut, the top composed of three deeply scalloped upright panels forming deep storage slots, the outside faces ornately incised w/scrolling band w/ebonized trim & a center roundel, raised on a U-form support joining a central post w/urn finial raised on four flat S-scroll legs w/line-incised decoration & ebonized trim, original finish, ca. 1880's, 12 x 18", 28" h. **$450**

Mission-style (Arts & Crafts movement) one-drawer stand, oak, a square top above a single narrow drawer w/turned wood pulls raised on tall square legs joined by a medial shelf, branded mark of Gustav Stickley, ca. 1912, 16" sq., 28 1/2" h. (ILLUS.) **$90,576**

Stools

Renaissance Revival Ebonized Stool

Stools are found in many furniture styles. Designed to be practical, many are found with painted finishes. Expect to find signs of usage, as many stools have served generations of users.

A place to rest one's weary feet made footstools very popular in many furniture periods. As the styles of furniture evolved, so did the decorations and finishes on stools.

A common type of stool is the round variety used to provide seating for someone playing a piano or organ. The more ornate the stool, the higher the value. Look for examples that have working mechanisms to raise and lower the top.

Another common type of stool is one that is used for seating. Some of these are primitive in nature, being made from materials at hand and often created to fit into a specified location. Look for a broader top on a stool designed to be used for seating.

Fine French Art Deco Stool

Art Deco stool, upholstered mahogany, a deep round cushion top on an upholstered apron & round wood frame w/beaded edge & scroll-carved turned legs, Sue et Mare, France, ca. 1925, 27" d., 18 1/2" h. (ILLUS.) **$6,325**

Bank teller stools, Modern style, oak, a rectangular top raised on four pairs of slender square supports joined by a narrow medial rail above the squared outswept lower legs w/square feet, one w/paper label "First Nationl Bank of Dwight," designed by Frank L. Smith Bank, Dwight, Illinois, 1908, 12 14 x 18 1/2", 27 & 28" h., pr. **$7,475**

Fine Chippendale Candlestand

Classical footstool, carved mahogany, the deep rectangular upholstered top above a deep cove-molded & bead-trimmed apron on a half-round band centered by a carved spread-winged eagle w/shield, leafy scroll-carved paw feet, ca. 1830, 24" l. **$2,185**

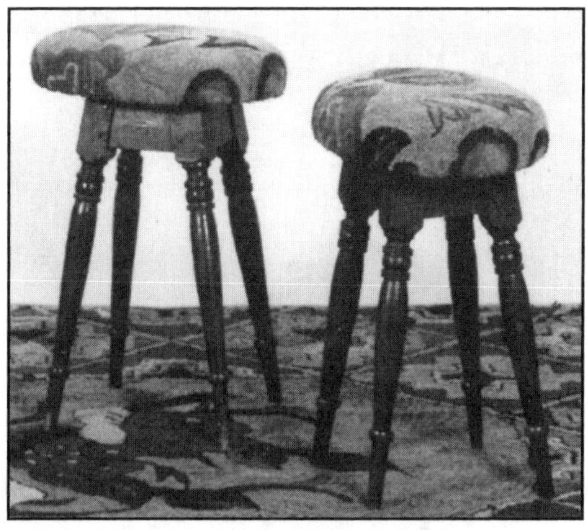

Country-style Stools with Round Tops

Country-style stools, stained wood, a round upholstered top raised on a canted apron raised on ring- and knob-turned reeded & canted legs, stained red, 19th c., pr. **$1,840**

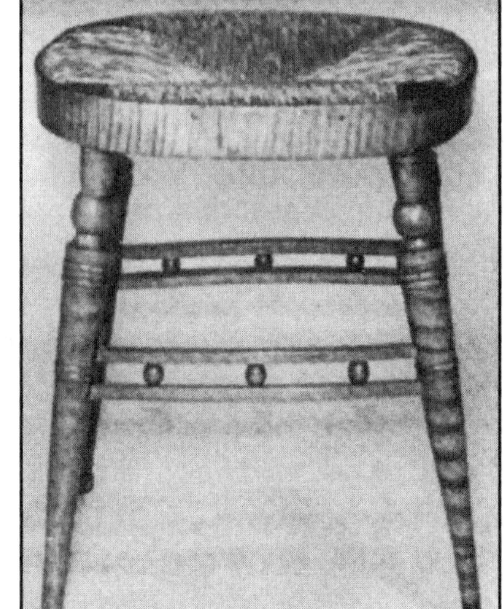

Federal Curly Maple Stool

Federal stool, curly maple, the oblong woven rush seat enclosed w/a wooden framework & raised on four ring-, knob- and rod-turned tapering canted legs joined by slender double stretchers separated by three spheres, early 19th c., 11 1/2 x 15", 16 1/4" h. **$1,980**

Golden Oak Adjustable Piano Stool

Piano stool, Victorian Golden Oak style, the tall gently flared back w/a wide shaped crest-rail w/corner scrolls on ring-turned stiles flanking five slender spindles all above the round adjustable seat, the seat platform raised on four ring- and knob-turned canted legs joined by ring-turned stretchers to a center ring-turned post, the legs ending in brass paws w/glass balls, original finish, ca. 1890s, seat 14" d., 36" h. **$300**

Early William & Mary Joint Stool

Queen Anne footstool, carved mahogany, the rectangular slip seat above a conforming frame, on cabriole legs w/shell-carved knees & stocking trifid feet, 18th c., 21" l., 16 1/2" h ..**$1,725**

Weaver's work stool, painted wood, tall w/a round hollowed seat frame w/woven leather seat on four reverse-tapering legs joined by turned stretchers, worn old red paint, New England, early 19th c., top 13 1/4" x 13 1/2", 28" h. **$920**

William & Mary joint stool, maple, the rectangular molded top overhanging an apron w/splayed block-, vase- and ring-turned legs on knob feet, joined by flat box stretchers, old refinish, probably Massachusetts, early 18th c., minor imperfections, 16 x 24", 23" h. (ILLUS.) **$8,050**

Windsor Painted Footstool

Windsor footstool, painted pine, the oval top w/incised edge raised on widely splayed bamboo-turned legs joined by turned box stretchers, painted white w/red trim, early-19th c., 9 1/2 x 15", 10 1/4" h. (ILLUS.) **$287**

Windsor stool, painted, a triangular top on three canted baluster- and ring-turned legs joined by swelled stretchers, old black paint, the top recovered w/worn hooked rug fragment, early 19th c., 13" h. **$550**

Tables

Arts & Crafts Library Table

Tables are present in every furniture style. Because they served a very useful purpose, they were treasured and frequently designed to serve a particular function. As furniture styles evolved and wealth increased, more and more of these specialized forms became fashionable.

A simple table suited the early settlers, one that functioned for food preparation and serving, as well as a gathering place. During the Federal decorating style, it was popular to keep all furniture, including tables, pushed against the wall of a room, so that the room could be multi-functional. Many tables from this period, including card, game, and tea tables, are hinged to help fold them even more compactly.

As decorating styles continued to evolve, more tables were introduced into the main part of a room, whether a dining room or living room. Tables to hold lamps and even telephones became pop-

Classical Tilt-top Center Table

ular as those wonderful inventions invaded American lifestyles and decorating themes.

To determine the age and style of a table, look carefully at all the elements, but pay close attention to the legs and feet. Often these are the easiest to identify. Claw and ball feet are distinctly Chippendale. While brasses are more ornamental than functional on tables, they also give clues as to age, if original to the table. Examination of construction techniques, nails, screws, etc., will often lead to more dating clues.

When purchasing an antique table, be sure to examine it carefully, checking for original parts, legs, leaves, and hardware. Often table legs have been shortened over the years, and sometimes leaves develop warps or may have been shortened.

Breakfast tables are typically small tables used to serve breakfast in either a bedroom or sitting room. They are found in most design periods during the era of big households and full staffs. Later design periods often dropped this style of table when breakfasts were served in the kitchen, dining room, etc.

During the times when elegant entertaining often included playing card games, a beautiful table served this purpose. Many card tables have folding tops, often to facilitate placing them near exterior walls when that style of decorating was popular. As cabinetmakers developed the form, more elaborate styles of tops evolved, leaving the plain rectangular version behind as D-shapes, ovolo corners, etc., became fashionable.

Games tables are small tables designed to be used to play parlor games. They are usually constructed with a shaped top so that those who use these tables can sit comfortably to play the game of their choice. Some game tables have interior wells to store pieces. Expect to find signs of usage around the edges of these tables and especially on any playing surface.

A center table is defined as a table used in the center of a room or hall and which is generally more formal, placed to display one's wealth and good taste.

The use of a small, lower table as a coffee table did not become popular until the Art Deco period. The Modernism Era designers carried the concept to new shapes.

Breakfast Tables

Classical Mahogany Breakfast Table

Classical breakfast table, carved & inlaid mahogany, the rectangular top w/brass inlay in outline & stamped brass on the edges of the flanking, shaped drop leaves above one working & one faux end apron drawer, drop pendants at the corners, raised on four ring-turned columns on a rectangular curve-edged platform raised on outswept leaf-carved legs ending in paw feet on casters, replaced pulls, old refinish, repairs, losses, New York City, ca. 1820-30, 24 x 39", 28" h. **$2,415**

Center Tables

Leleu Art Deco Center Table

Art Deco center table, mahogany, a rounded top above a heavy squared cross-form pedestal on four cross-form downswept feet, designed by Jules Leleu, France, ca. 1925, 40" d., 29" h. **$8,050**

Classical Center Table on Casters

Classical center table, carved & veneered mahogany, the round top w/rounded edge above a conforming apron w/applied panels & cast-brass beaded edge, raised on a ring-turned & acanthus leaf-carved post on four outswept scrolled & acanthus-carved legs ending in cast-brass cap caster feet, refinished, minor imperfections, probably Massachusetts, ca. 1825, 36" d., 27 1/2" h. **$8,050**

Victorian Rococo Parlor Center Table

Victorian Rococo parlor center table, carved rosewood, a white marble turtle-top above a serpentine molded apron deeply carved on all sides w/a spray of flowers & fruit, raised on four incurved cabriole legs carved to match & joined by a pierced foliate-carved X-form stretcher centered by an urn filled w/nuts & w/a turned finial, on casters, ca. 1850, 30 1/2 x 42 3/4", 30" h. **$2,880**

Coffee Tables

Fine Art Deco Coffee Table

Art Deco coffee table, ormolu-mounted mahogany, a rectangular dished top w/beaded edge raised on an inset frieze above the rectangular frame w/thin ormolu angular mounts at the center apron & raised on tapering curved squared legs ending in brass feet, Jules Leleu, France, ca. 1935, 18 x 30", 15" h. **$7,475**

Chippendale-Style Coffee Table

Chippendale-Style coffee table, carved mahogany, the rectangular white marble top w/molded serpentine edges above the leafy scroll-carved apron, raised on cabriole legs w/leaf-carved knees & ending in claw-and-ball feet, original finish, ca. 1920-40, 18 x 32", 18" h. **$450**

Danish Modern coffee table, walnut, long narrow rectangular top w/rounded corners raised on four tapering cylindrical legs, signed w/metal tag "Illums Bolighus," Copenhagen, Denmark, ca. 1950, 19 3/4 x 60", 16" h. **$201**

Fine Modern Style Coffee Table

Modern style coffee table, maple, glass & brass, the long tapering oval plate glass top raised on a widely flaring V-shaped maple three-part support w/a pair of forked legs at the front & tiny brackets at the back, an oval plate glass medial shelf, designed by Carlo Mollino, manufactured by Singer and Company, New York, glass shelves acid-etched "Secuisit," ca. 1952, 24 1/2 x 50 1/2", 16" h. (ILLUS.) **$19,550**

Modern style coffee table, patinated bronze, the round top cast in low-relief w/Chinese figures in a landscape, raised on round-section legs headed by brackets & ending in casters, signed by Philip La Verne, 1950s, 45" d., 17" h. **$176**

Dining Tables

Fine Art Deco Dining Table

Art Deco dining table, figured mahogany, the round top w/a rayed mahogany design raised on a heavy wood column on a nickel band raised on three low arched splayed legs w/nickeled feet, attributed to Jules Leleu, France, ca. 1930, 42" d., 22" h. (ILLUS.) **$14,950**

Art Deco dining table, rosewood, the rectangular top w/two draw-leaf extensions above downswept supports on a flaring plinth, France, ca. 1925, 36 x 61", 30" h. (missing leaves, uneven finish) **$1,955**

Arts & Crafts Round Dining Table

Art Deco dining table, walnut, the round top w/a sunburst pattern overhanging a narrow apron raised on five slender turned & tapering legs w/wide disks near the top, France, ca. 1935, 63" d., 30" h. **$5,750**

Arts & Crafts dining table, oak, an expandable round top above a conforming apron, supported on a square tapering pedestal pierce-carved w/stylized fleur-de-lis cut-outs, raised on a curve-sided platform base w/curved corbels on casters, late 19th - early 20th c., minor stains & scratches, 48" d., 30 3/4" h. (ILLUS.) **$805**

Fine Classical Dining Table

Classical dining table, carved & veneered mahogany, extension-type, round top w/molded edge over a smooth apron w/thin gadrooned base band raised on a clustered column-form split pedestal ending in four downswept foliate-carved legs ending in paw feet on casters, together w/seven leaves, New York City, ca. 1840, closed 48" d., 29 1/2" h. (ILLUS.) **$7,475**

Classical dining table, carved & veneered mahogany, a rectangular overhanging top flanked by deep rounded leaves over a straight beaded apron w/a small drawer at each end, raised on

Danish Modern Dining Table

two lyre-form supports centering a carved fan w/applied brass rosettes on molded arched & outswept molded legs ending in cast-brass hairy paw feet, ring-turned & beaded square medial stretchers, old refinish, probably New England, ca. 1820, open 50 x 51 1/2", 28 3/4" h. **$2,990**

Danish Modern dining table, walnut, a wide rectangular top flanked by wide half-round drop leaves, raised on four plain turned & slightly tapering legs, w/one leaf insert, designed by Hans Wegner, Denmark, ca. 1950 (ILLUS.) **$863**

Early 20th Century Oak Dining Table

Early 20th century dining table, quarter-sawn oak, round top above a plain apron, raised on a heavy turned pedestal w/four projecting heavy scroll legs, on casters, refinished, ca. 1910, 48" d., 30" h. (ILLUS.) **$1,200**

Federal dining table, mahogany & mahogany veneer, three-part, D-form and sections on conforming aprons w/cock-beaded edges joining four vase- and ring-turned slightly swelled reeded legs topped by veneered dies & ending in applied brass ball feet, flanking a central rectangular top w/deep hinged drop leaves on a deeply recessed straight apron joining six tapering square legs,

Federal Country Dining Table

two of which swing out, old surface, Philadelphia, ca. 1810-15, open 54 x 122", 28 3/4" h. (minor repairs) **$9,200**

Federal country-style dining table, tiger stripe maple, the rectangular top flanked by wide hinged drop leaves over a plain apron & six ring- and rod-turned legs w/small bun feet, old refinish, no casters, New England, ca. 1825, 29 x 56 1/2", 28" h. (ILLUS.) **$3,335**

Jacobean-Style Dining Table

Federal dining table, mahogany, two-part, each half of demilune form w/a molded edge & a wide hinged drop leaf, wide plain conforming apron, each half w/four reeded & ring-turned legs w/ball feet, one leg a swing-out support for the leaf, Massachusetts, probably Newburyport, late 18th to early 19th c., open 48 x 90", 30" h. **$7,188**

Jacobean-Style dining table, inlaid walnut, draw-leaf extension-type, the rectangular top w/draw-leaf extensions above an S-scroll-carved apron w/scroll-carved brackets above the bulbous carved cup-and-cover design legs on shaped shoe feet joined by a half-round stretcher, some wear, ca. 1900, 35 x 71 1/2", 31" h. (ILLUS.) **$8,625**

Early Queen Anne Dining Table

Queen Anne dining table, carved & figured walnut, the rectangular top flanked by deep rectangular drop leaves, arched end aprons on cabriole legs ending in paneled trifid feet, appears to retain an old & possibly original finish, warm nut-brown color, Pennsylvania, ca. 1750, closed 17 1/2 x 50 1/2", 28" h. **$4,887**

Late Victorian Round Dining Table

Victorian Baroque Revival dining table, mahogany, the round expandable top w/narrow gadrooned rim band & deep apron raised on a heavy round pedestal w/the ribbed lower section surrounded by four large carved lions heads over leaf-carved scrolls continuing into extended legs ending in paw feet, old mellow alligatored finish, w/five leaves, minor wear, late 19th c., 59 1/2" d., 29 1/2" h. (ILLUS.) **$5,225**

Victorian Baroque Revival dining table, oak, expandable, the divided round top w/a deep apron decorated w/applied leaf carving & a beaded lower edge raised on five heavy ring-turned & tapering block supports w/carved leafy scroll decoration raised on a heavy H-form flattened stretcher w/arched & scroll-carved

Oak Dining Table with Dolphins

crested paw foot, original finish, ca. 1895, w/five leaves, 48" d., 30" h. **$3,000**

Victorian Golden Oak dining table, quarter-sawn oak, expandable, the divided square top over a deep flat apron w/incised bands & carved scrolls at each corner, raised on four heavy ring-, reeded baluster- and block-turned legs & a pair of slender ring- and baluster-turned inner supports, the legs joined by heavy carved stretchers topped by a high rounded panel flanked by carved figural dolphins, refinished, w/six leaves, ca. 1910, 54" w. closed, 30" h. (ILLUS.) **$3,300**

Victorian Dining Table with Ornate Legs

Victorian Renaissance Revival dining table, mahogany, expandable, the round divided top w/a deep apron carved w/scroll trim, raised on a heavy octagonal split pedestal w/half-round knob-turned spindles on panels alternating w/heavy S-scroll outswept legs carved w/beads, panels & roundels, on casters, original finish, w/six leaves, ca. 1875, 48" d., 30" h. (ILLUS.) .... **$1,800-$2,000**

Victorian Renaissance Revival dining table, walnut & burl walnut, expandable, the divided square top w/rounded corners above a deep apron w/burl trim & burl end panels, raised on a

Victorian Rococo Dining Table

heavy octagonal central post w/burl trim surrounded by four heavy scroll-cut outswept legs w/burl roundels & panels, on casters, refinished, closed 50" w., 30" h. **$3,500**

Victorian Rococo dining table, carved walnut, divided expandable top, the round top w/molded edges & deep apron raised on four baluster-turned & scroll-carved legs & long carved scrolling supports tapering toward the top center & joined by a heavy leaf-carved cross-stretcher centered by a heavy center post w/an acanthus leaf-carved band, five original leaves w/case, original dark finish, ca. 1860, 60" d. closed, 30" h. (ILLUS.) .. **$7,000**

Early William & Mary Dining Table

William & Mary dining table, maple, gate-leg type, a rectangular top w/rounded ends flanked by wide rounded drop leaves forming an oval top above an apron on six block-, ring- and baluster-turned legs joined by block-, ring- and baluster-turned stretchers, flattened knob feet, refinished, imperfections, Massachusetts, early 18th c., open 41 1/2 x 52 1/4", 22" h. **$9,775**

Dressing Tables

Majorelle Art Nouveau Dressing Table

Art Nouveau dressing table, carved mahogany, "Les Lilas" patt., the large squared upright mirror within a foliate-carved frame flanked by flaring stained side panels, above a central plateau w/raised ends over two pairs of small drawers flanking an arched kneehole, gilt-bronze mounts, raised on slender & slightly curved foliate-carved legs, Louis Majorelle, France, ca. 1900, 22 1/2 x 49", 62 1/2" h. **$4,140**

Chippendale Walnut Dressing Table

Chippendale dressing table, walnut, the rectangular top w/molded edge & shaped front corners overhanging a case w/a long drawer over three small lip-molded drawers, deeply scalloped apron, raised on cabriole legs ending in trifid feet, butterfly brasses, Delaware Valley, 18th c., 21 1/4 x 35 1/4", 29 1/2" h. **$5,175**

Classical Country Dressing Table

Classical country-style dressing table, painted & decorated, the scroll-cut crestboard behind a small rectangular drawer on the rectangular top overhanging an apron w/a single long drawer, raised on slender ring- and rod-turned tapering legs w/peg feet, original red & brown graining simulating rosewood w/yellow foliate designs on the leg corner blocks & overall yellow-painted bordering to simulate inlay, Maine, early 19th c., 17 3/4 x 34", 34 1/2" h. **$1,150**

Haywood-Wakefield Dressing Table

Modern style dressing table, mahogany, a high pointed arch mirror above a tapering rectangular top on conforming open compartment at one end w/a quarter-round rank of three drawers w/long wooden pulls at the opposite end, on tapering bracket feet, champagne finish, mark of Haywood-Wakefield, Model No. M586, ca. 1955, 19 1/4 x 50", 62 3/4" h. **$345**

Queen Anne Dressing Table

Queen Anne dressing table, maple & pine, rectangular top w/molded edges above an apron w/a pair of deep drawers flanking a small shallow central drawer above a deeply scalloped apron w/two urn-turned drops, simple cabriole legs ending in pad feet, rear knee return missing, formerly painted white, New England, 1740-60, 18 1/2 x 34 1/2", 29 1/2" h. **$3,737**

End Tables

Colonial Revial Mahogany End Table

Colonial Revival end table, mahogany & mahogany veneer, a rectangular top w/molded edges & carved projecting corner stiles flanking a bow-front case w/three narrow graduated drawers w/ornate brass pulls, raised on simple cabriole legs w/leaf-carved knees ending in peg feet, early 20th c., 15 x 22", 30" h. **$800**

Game Tables

Chippendale Games Table

Chippendale games table, mahogany & mahogany veneer, folding turret-top style w/deep rounded corners & scalloped aprons w/fan-carved drops, raised on cabriole legs w/shell-carved knees & ending in paw feet **$3,750**

Fine Classical Card Table

Classical card table, carved mahogany & mahogany veneer, the rectangular folding top above a conforming frieze w/beaded edge on a tapering pedestal carved around the lower half w/bold acanthus leaves & basket of fruit on a shaped concave platform w/acanthus leaf-carved paw feet on casters, Philadelphia area, ca. 1825, refinished, 18 1/2 x 38", 30 1/4" h. **$4,888**

Federal Inlaid Mahogany Card Table

Federal card tables, inlaid mahogany, the half-round hinged top w/flattened slightly projecting front section above a conforming apron w/a long oval inlaid reserve at the front flanked by line-inlaid blocks, raised on four square tapering slender legs, early 19th c., pr. (ILLUS. of one) **$12,100**

Victorian Tilt-top Games Table

Victorian Renaissance Revival games table, walnut, burl walnut & maple, the rounded dished top w/a wide molded border around walnut burl panels centered by a diamond-shaped inlaid checkerboard, tilting & pivoting above a slender turned pedestal on a tripod base w/outswept scroll-cut legs mounted w/roundels, ca. 1875, refinished, 22" d., 30" h. **$450**

Hutch Tables

Rectangular Hutch Table

Hutch (or chair) table, painted pine, the rectangular cleated top w/old red paint tilting above wide sides & closed back over seat w/narrow apron, low cut-out feet, original red surface, minor surface imperfections, New England, early 19th c., 36 x 43", 27 1/2" h. **$3,220**

Lamp Tables

Classical Revival Oak Lamp Table

Classical Revival lamp table, oak & quarter-sawn oak veneer, the round top raised on a heavy squared baluster-form pedestal w/a stepped square base resting on a squared platform on C-scroll feet, refinished, ca. 1910, 20" d., 30" h. **$350**

Colonial Revival Oak Lamp Table

Colonial Revival lamp table, oak, a four-lobed top overhanging a deep apron w/arched base raised on four ring-turned reeded legs joined by a medial four-lobed shelf, on baluster- and knob-turned feet, original finish, ca. 1890s, 20" w., 30" h. **$400**

Library Tables

Early Bentwood Library Table

Bentwood library table, mahogany, rectangular w/reeded edges above a bentwood double-loop trestle base w/top scrolls & flaring leg bases on arched stretchers on bun feet, by J. & J. Kohn, Austria, ca. 1910, wear, 24 x 40", 29 1/2" h. **$690**

Limbert Mission Oak Library Table

Mission-style (Arts & Crafts movement) library table, oak, a wide rectangular top overhanging a case w/two-tiered end open shelves w/vertical slats at each end & joined by a single long drawer over a lower medial stretcher shelf, original finish, branded Charles Limbert mark, Model No. 106, ca. 1907, 29 1/2 x 48", 29 1/2" h. (ILLUS.) **$1,380**

Mission-style (Arts & Crafts movement) library table, oak, rectangular top above an apron w/a row of three drawers w/metal plates & looped pulls, square stile legs joined by a cross strecher w/wide upright splat & a medial wide shelf, red decal & paper label of Gustav Stickley, Model No. 659, ca. 1909, 31 3/4 x 53 7/8", 29 3/4" h. **$7,475**

Fine English Baroque Revival Table

Victorian Baroque Revival library table, carved walnut, a long rectangular top w/molded edges above a deep apron carved w/scrolled gadrooning raised on heavy shell- and fruit-carved tapering supports on shoe feet ending w/carved recumbent lions, the ends joined by a carved trestle stretcher w/baluster-turned spindles, England, late 19th c. **$3,000**

Parlor Tables

Baroque Revival Parlor Table

Baroque Revival parlor table, walnut veneer, the octagonal top w/fanned veneering centered by an inlaid floral medallion over a deep carved apron raised on four legs w/ornate scroll carving at the top & feet & joined by a quatrefoil-form stretcher w/central rosette, early 20th c., 30" d., 29" h. **$345**

Eastlake Marble-topped Parlor Table

Victorian Eastlake parlor table, walnut, the white rectangular molded top w/molded edges above a flat apron w/incised bands of flowerheads & angled carved drop corners, raised on four flat scallop-carved & line-incised outswept legs joined by short flat double stretchers to a ring-turned central post, on casters, refinished, ca. 1880, 20 x 30", 30" h. **$600**

Fine Turtle-top Parlor Table

Victorian Renaissance Revival parlor center table, rosewood, oblong white marble turtle-top above a conforming panel-carved serpentine apron raised on four S-scroll-carved legs joined by double S-scroll-carved cross stretchers joined in the center by a post w/a large urn-carved finial, ca. 1850-60 (ILLUS.) **$3,000**

Victorian Renaissance Revival parlor table, inlaid, gilt-incised & ebonized rosewood, the rectangular top w/wide rounded ends centered by an oblong satinwood-inlaid floral reserve surrounded by a wide band of inlaid burl, the raised molded edges w/an ebonized band raised on a conforming apron w/gilt line-incised central panels, raised on four knob- and ring-turned reeded & ebonized tapering legs joined by a flattened trestle-form stretcher w/gilt line incising & centered by an ebonized & gilt-trimmed carved central urn finial, original brass casters, original finish, ca. 1875, 22 x 36", 30" h. **$2,500**

Rare & Fine Meeks Parlor Table

Victorian Rococo parlor table, laminated carved rosewood, white marble turtle-top on a molded conforming frame w/a deep arched floral- and fruit-carved pierced apron raised on four flower- and leaf-carved cabriole legs w/scroll & peg feet on brass casters, arched pierced-carved cross stretcher centered by a large carved urn of fruit over gadroon-carved bands & pierced scroll carving, J. & J. W. Meeks, New York City, ca. 1855 .... **$31,350**

Pembroke Tables

Inlaid Cherry Pembroke Table

Federal Pembroke table, inlaid cherry, rectangular top w/rounded ends flanked by half-round drop leaves w/incised beaded edges above a conforming skirt w/an end drawer, the lower edge inlaid w/contrasting stringing, on four square tapering legs w/icicle inlay, stringing & banded cuffs, original drawer handle, old refinish, minor imperfections, probably Rhode Island, ca. 1800, 32 3/4 x 36 3/4", 27 3/4" h. **$7,475**

Pier Tables

Classical Mahogany Pier Table

Classical pier table, carved mahogany & mahogany veneer, a rectangular black marble top w/rounded edges above a veneered frieze w/banded edges above a pier mirror flanked by heavy scrolled & fan-carved supports on a conformingly shaped platform joined by an incurved shelf, on four turned feet, original finish, Boston, ca. 1825, imperfections, 19 1/4 x 38", 33 3/4" h. **$2,760**

Side Tables

Unique Baroque Revival Side Table

Baroque Revival side table, walnut, the octagonal top w/a line-inlaid border raised on four tall finely carved standing egrets resting on figural carved rams heads on a scalloped cross-form platform w/center finial & raised on curved blocked & reeded feet, original finish, ca. 1920, 20" w., 30" h. **$2,400**

Chippendale-Style Oak Side Table

Chippendale-Style side table, oak, the large round top w/a molded edge raised on a baluster-turned & acanthus leaf-carved pedestal on four splayed cabriole legs ending in bold paw feet, refinished, ca. 1900, 22" d., 30" h. **$450**

Federal-Style side table, mahogany & mahogany veneer, the delicate superstructure w/a narrow rectangular top w/low serpentine gallery raised on end cross-form supports & a solid back

Delicate Federal-Style Side Table

w/fine crock-grain veneer above the small rectangular top w/molded edges above a case w/a pair of cross-banded drawers over a long drawer all w/small round brass pulls, the case w/bail end handles, raised on ring-turned & reeded slender legs w/tapering outswept feet, original finish, ca. 1910, 15 x 22", 42" h. **$650**

Louis XV-Style Marquetry Side Table

Louis XV-Style side table, gilt-bronze mounted tulipwood marquetry, the shaped rectangular top veneered w/a flower-filled basket & sprays of flowers within a brass banding, above a single frieze drawer, the drawer & apron sides similarly inlaid w/flowers, raised on simple cabriole legs w/gilt-bronze knee mounts & sabots, France, late 19th c., 16 x 27", 28" h. **$6,600**

Stickley Brothers Quaint Side Table

Mission-style (Arts & Crafts movement) side table, oak, a round top above a square narrow apron on four slender square legs w/through-tenon cross stretchers, original finish, Quaint metal tag of the Stickley Brothers, Model No. 2500, 24" d., 30" h. **$990**

Fine Napolean III Side Table

Napolean III side table, marquetry & burl, square top w/ornate central marquetry squared panel framed by ornate scrolling above four D-form burl-banded & marquetry scroll-decorated drop leaves, on gilt-metal-mounted turned & tapering legs w/ring-turned peg feet joined by a curved cross stretcher centered by an urn-form finial, France, late 19th c., 21" sq., 30" h. **$2,300**

Queen Anne-Style Side Table

Queen Anne-Style side table, walnut, a round tan marble top w/a long pierced brass gallery raised on a reeded turned & tapering pedestal on a tripod base w/simple cabriole legs ending in pad feet on casters, ca. 1920, 24" d., 25" h. **$300**

Golden Oak Square Side Table

Victorian Eastlake side table, walnut, a rectangular top w/molded edges above a deep apron w/a narrow central burl panel flanked by incised line bands & a scroll-cut edge band on each side, raised on a cluster of four slender flat rectangular line-incised legs flaring out at the bottom & on porcelain casters, the legs centered by a baluster- and ring-turned post joined to them by a short cross stretcher, ca. 1890, 20 1/2 x 28", 31 1/4" h. **$358**

Victorian Golden Oak side table, the square top w/a slightly serpentine edge above a narrow apron, raised on four slightly canted sausage-turned legs joined by a squared serpentine medial rail & ending in brass claw & glass ball feet, original finish, ca. 1900, 22" w., 30" h. (ILLUS.) **$300**

Early Windsor Side Table

Victorian Renaissance Revival side table, walnut & burl walnut, the oval white marble top w/molded edges above a deep molded apron, raised on a short heavy baluster-turned post w/a beaded band above four scroll-carved supports above arched & flaring flat legs w/curved raised burl panels & centering a turned bowl-form finial, original casters, original finish, ca. 1870, 16 x 22", 30" h. **$500**

Windsor side table, painted pine, a scrubbed rectangular top w/breadboard ends widely overhanging four slightly canted rod- and baluster-turned legs joined by upper & lower box stretchers, legs w/red staining, top w/old natural finish, New England, early 19th c., 20 1/4 x 29 1/2", 26 1/2" h. (ILLUS.) **$2,415**

Sofa Tables

Fine Classical Sofa Table

Classical sofa table, mahogany & mahogany inlaid veneer, the rectangular overhanging reeded top w/two rounded end drop leaves above an apron w/one faux & one working cockbeaded string-inlaid drawer on each side, raised on a ring-turned pedestal & concave platform above outswept curving legs ending in cast foliate brass casters, appears to retain original ivory pulls, Rhode Island, ca. 1810-15, imperfections, open 35 1/2 x 55 1/2", 29 1/4" h. **$6,900**

Unusual Federal Sofa Table

Federal sofa table, figured maple, the rectangular long top w/reeded edges flanked by D-form drop leaves above an apron w/a long cockbeaded drawer w/two oval brass pulls, on slender ring- and rod-turned legs w/knob ankles & peg feet, appears to retain original hardware, probably New England, early 19th c., 29 3/4 x 44 3/4", 29" h. **$4,887**

Fine Regency Sofa Table

Regency sofa table, rosewood, a rectangular top w/rounded corners & rounded edges slightly overhanging a conforming apron w/a beaded lower edge, raised on ring-, knob & baluster-turned & reeded end legs on blocked cross bars on bun feet, England, early 19th c. **$4,000**

Tavern Tables

Early Stained Tavern Table

Tavern table, country-style, stained pine & maple, the long rectangular top w/breadboard ends overhanging an apron w/a long single drawer & simple wood knob, raised on baluster-, ring- and block-turned legs joined by a block-, ring & sausage-turned H-stretcher, on turned tapering feet, old surface, alterations, probably Mid-Atlantic States, 18th c., dark stain, 23 1/2 x 37", 26 1/4" h. **$2,875**

Federal Country-style Tavern Table

Federal country-style tavern table, maple, the rectangular breadboard top widely overhanging an apron w/a single long drawer raised on slender square tapering legs, old surface w/vestiges of dark brown paint, possibly southeastern New England, ca. 1800, 25 x 36", 27 3/4" h. (ILLUS.) **$2,875**

Federal country-style tavern table, painted pine & maple, a long rectangular top w/breadboard ends overhanging a deep apron joining four square tapering legs, old red paint on base, New England, ca. 1790-1810, 28 x 46", 28" h. (imperfections) **$2,530**

Quality Queen Anne Tavern Table

Queen Anne country-style tavern table, maple, rectangular two-board top w/notched corners cleaned & w/old finish w/stains, widely overhanging a deep flat mortised & pinned apron on turned tapered legs ending in duck feet, old red on the base, 18th c., 26 1/2 x 36", 27 1/2" h. (minor old age crack in top) **$5,500**

Queen Anne tavern table, painted pine, oval top widely overhangs a deep apron on splayed ring- and rod-turned tapering legs ending in turned feet, scrubbed top, original red paint on base, minor imperfections, New England, 18th c., 26 3/8 x 35", 26 1/4" h. (ILLUS.) **$14,950**

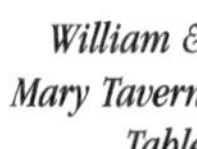

William & Mary Tavern Table

William & Mary tavern table, painted birch & pine, the oval overhanging top rests on four splayed slender baluster- and ring-turned legs continuing to turned feet & joined by a straight apron & box stretchers, painted black, probably New England, mid-18th c., imperfections, 24 x 33", 17" h. (ILLUS.) .. **$8,050**

William & Mary tavern table, pine & birch, the oval top above a deep canted apron w/a single drawer raised on canted baluster- and ring-turned legs ending in blocks joined by box stretchers & raised on waisted knob feet, retains traces of red wash, New England, 1700-30, diminutive size, 17 1/4" x 25 1/2", 25" h. **$12,650**

Tea Tables

English Chippendale Tea Table

Chippendale tea table, carved mahogany, a round top supported on a dovetailed mahogany box open at both ends rotating above a baluster-form pedestal carved w/diamonds enclosing scratch-carved details on a tripod base w/cabriole legs carved at the knees w/acanthus leaves & ending in ball-and-claw feet, old surface, repairs, England, late 18th c., 32 1/4" d., 29" h. **$2,415**

Queen Anne Country Tea Table

Chippendale tea table, mahogany, round one-board dished top above a pedestal w/a turned columnar section above a baluster-turned lower section, on a tripod base w/cabriole legs ending in snake feet, old mellow finish, attributed to Newport, Rhode Island, 18th c., 23 1/2" d., 27 5/8" h. (restoration, pieced repairs, filled holes in top from a larger cleat). **$8,575**

Queen Anne country-style tea table, maple & pine, the rectangular breadboard top widely overhanging a valanced apron w/a single long drawer, raised on four cabriole legs ending in pad feet, old refinish, top of different origin, other imperfections, New England, 18th c., 26 x 38 1/4", 27" h. (ILLUS.) **$2,875**

Work Tables

Classcial Work Table

Classical work table, carved mahogany & mahogany veneer, the rectangular top flanked by two wide D-form drop leaves above the deep apron w/two round-fronted drawers w/simple turned wood pulls, on a heavy square tapering pedestal w/a stepped base on the cross-form platform raised on scrolled leaf carving & paw feet on casters, refinished, attributed to Isaac Vose and Son, Boston, ca. 1825, closed 21 x 22", 30 1/2" h. **$2,875**

Federal Maple Work Table

Federal country-style work table, tiger stripe & bird's-eye maple, a rectangular top flanked by rounded wide drop leaves above a deep apron w/two drawers w/small brass knobs, on ring-, baluster- and rod-turned legs ending in knob feet, replaced brasses, refinished, probably New York, ca. 1825, 17 x 24", 28" h. **$805**

Wardrobes & Armoires

French Provincial Carved Armoire

For early settlers, a simple cupboard usually did the job of storing clothing, along with a chest of drawers or perhaps a blanket chest. That was all the storage needed for their small wardrobes. The huge walk-in closets of today's modern homes would certainly astound our ancestors.

Armoires, chifforobes, and wardrobes are all types of cupboards created for the storage of clothing.

Fine Victorian Golden Oak Wardrobe

As the name implies, an armoire is a large cupboard. The form was first popular with French furniture makers. A few American styles included large cupboards that served as clothing storage. Many European forms of armoires are sold and used by Americans and Canadians.

Chifforobe—what a wonderful name for a cupboard to store clothes, hats, and accessories. American furniture designers of the 20th century added mirrors to these handy armoire-type cupboards, giving their furniture one more function.

Wardrobe is the common name for a large cupboard designed to hold clothes. Each geographical region put their distinctive signature on handmade wardrobes.

French Art Deco Armoire

Armoire, Art Deco, mahogany & bird's-eye maple, the shaped rectangular top above a pair of wide doors set w/copper looping handles & opening to an interior w/mirror, shelves & drawers, all raised on a shaped, stepped plinth, in the manner of Dominique, France, ca. 1935, 19 x 62", 78" h. **$2,875**

Early Biedermeier Armoire

Armoire, Biedermeier, mahogany, the stepped rectangular top over a flaring graduated cornice over a pair of tall three-panel cupboard doors opening to later shelves, restoration, Europe, early 19th c., 21 x 49", 76" h. **$3,450**

Elegant Classical Armoire

Armoire, Classical, mahogany & mahogany veneer, the rectangular top w/a widely flaring deep ogee cornice above a frieze band w/ormolu figural swan mounts above a pair of tall paneled doors flanked by half-round columns w/acanthus leaf & scroll carvings & ormolu mounts, flat rounded front feet w/mounts, early 19th c., 19 x 60", 90" h. **$2,200**

French Provincial Carved Armoire

Armoire, French Provincial, oak, a rectangular top w/a widely flaring deep stepped cornice w/carved geometric frieze bands centered by pierce-carved central blocks, birds & grapevines above a pair of tall paneled doors w/grapevine carved panels at the top & base of each & long narrow brass strap hardware, a long carved pilaster between the doors, the deep scalloped apron carved w/further grapevines & a central floral medallion, short scroll front feet, France, 19th c., 18 x 72", 88" h. **$2,415**

Louis XV-Style Oak Armoire

Armoire, Louis XV-Style, oak, a rectangular top w/rounded corners on the deep, widely flaring stepped cornice above a leaf-carved frieze band centered by a carved basket above a pair of tall doors w/scroll and floral vine top border over an asymmetrical glazed panel above a medial band of leafy scroll carving above the lower solid panel, the sides w/three square panels, raised on a molded plinth on square feet, w/the original oak panels for the glazed door sections, France, 19th c., 24 x 60", 87" h. **$3,450**

Fine Aesthetic Movement Armoire

Armoire, Victorian Aesthetic Movement substyle, walnut & burl walnut, a high upright crestrail composed of roundels over carved points w/roundel-topped corner blocks, a deep stepped & flaring cornice above a single tall burl paneled door flanked by reeded pilasters w/small florette-carved panels, a narrow burl veneered bottom drawer w/brass bar & ring pulls, deep molded front molding, paneled sides, opens to a single top shelf, refinished, original hardware, last quarter 19th c., 20 x 38", 7' 6" h. **$2,800**

Victorian Rococo Armoire

Armoire, Victorian Rococo substyle, walnut w/faux rosewood graining, the rectangular top w/a wide arched front & deep ogee cornice over a large central frieze panel w/ornate carved leafy scrolls over a pair of tall arch-paneled doors w/brass pulls above a pair of bottom drawers w/carved trim, scallop-carved apron, bracket feet, refinished, demountable, ca. 1860, 16 x 45", 7' 6" h. **$2,400**

Art Deco Style Wardrobe

Wardrobe, Art Deco, oak, a flat rectangular top above a plain case w/a large tall flat door on the left & two shorter flat doors on the right, one side opens to a clothes rack, the two doors fitted w/four slide-out shelves, light finish, Bauhaus influenced design, Germany, ca. 1930, wear, scratches, 23 3/4 x 53", 71 1/2" h. **$460**

Fine Classical Wardrobe

Wardrobe, Classical, mahogany veneer, the wide rectangular top w/a deep stepped & flaring cornice above a pair of large tall two-panel doors opening to an interior w/veneered drawers, molded base on simple bracket feet, paneled sides, some small interior drawers added, other minor imperfections, mid-Atlantic states, ca. 1840, 26 x 65", 79 1/2" h. **$3,105**

Painted Country-style Wardrobe

Wardrobe, country-style, painted pine & poplar, a rectangular thick top above a tall two-panel off-center door above a single bottom drawer, molded flat base, pottery knob on door, wood knobs on drawer, interior fitted w/14 small cast-iron hooks & replaced shelf, old brown repaint, 19th c., age crack in door, top 19 x 39 3/4", 83 1/2" h. **$523**

Gustav Stickley Mission Wardrobe

Wardrobe, Mission-style (Arts & Crafts movement), oak, a rectangular top above a pair of tall double-paneled doors w/a small panel over a tall panel, copper V-pulls, interior fitted w/two open compartments over four long drawers above two open shelves, gently arched apron, red decal & paper Craftsman label of Gustav Stickley, Model No. 920, ca. 1910, some wear, small losses to wood at top, 16 1/2 x 34", 59 3/4" h. **$14,950**

Fine Aesthetic Movement Wardrobe

Wardrobe, Victorian Aesthetic Movement style, walnut & burl walnut, the rectangular top w/a high stepped front crest w/a geometric band above panels of bold scroll & leaf carving above a frieze band w/burl panels & leaf-carved blocks over a pair of tall panels & finely burled doors flanked by narrow side burl bands, two burled drawers at the bottom w/stamped brass pulls, molded flat base on thin block feet, refinished, demountable, ca. 1880s, 20 x 46", 8' h. **$2,800**

Simple Victorian Country Wardrobe

Wardrobe, Victorian country-style, walnut, a rectangular top w/a narrow molded cornice over a single tall double-panel door opening to a fitted rod above a single deep bottom drawer, simple bracket feet, one-board sides, door edge strip w/pieced repairs, found in Missouri, mid-19th c., 17 3/4 x 32", 73" h. **$1,650**

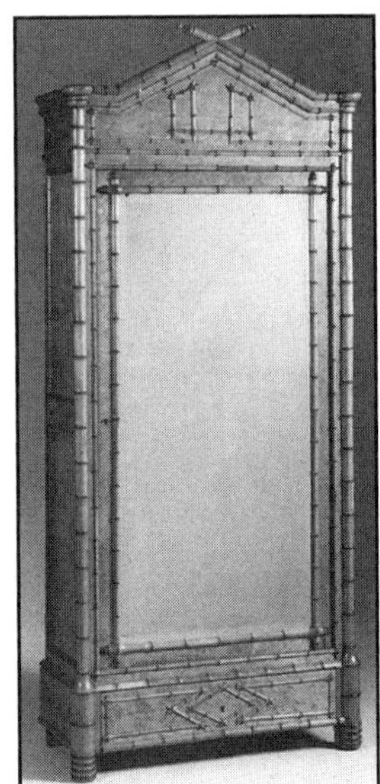

Victorian Faux Bamboo Wardrobe

Wardrobe, Victorian faux bamboo-style, bird's-eye maple, the pedimented top outlined w/ bamboo-turned trim forming a forked finial above a deep frieze band w/applied bamboo-turned panels over the tall mirrored door framed w/bamboo turnings & opening to shelves, flanked by bamboo-turned stiles, a bamboo-turned medial rail over the single bottom drawer w/further applied bamboo turnings, side stiles continue down to form round feet, America, second half 19th c., 17 3/4 x 40", 92" h. **$3,162**

Elaborate Golden Oak Wardrobe

Wardrobe, Victorian Golden Oak style, the high arched top crestrail decorated w/ornate scroll carving & a central flower head & rounded corners above a pair of tall paneled cupboard doors w/scroll-carved trim flanked by corner columns & centered by a small vertical rectangular beveled mirror above a flat serpentine panel, a bow-fronted base w/two drawers w/pierced-brass pulls flanked by leaf-carved feet, original dark finish, ca. 1900, 22 x 48", 7' 10" h. **$2,800**

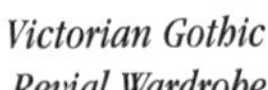

Victorian Gothic Revial Wardrobe

Wardrobe, Victorian Gothic Revival substyle, walnut, the rectangular top w/a deep flaring cornice over a pair of tall cupboard doors w/Gothic Arch panels over a single long drawer at the bottom, scalloped front apron, ca. 1865, 16 x 42", 73" h. **$690**

Victorian Rococo Walnut Wardrobe

Wardrobe, Victorian Rococo substyle, walnut, the high arched & scroll-carved front cornice w/a pair of lobed center cut-outs over a molded cornice above a pair of tall arch-paneled doors w/scroll-carved top corners, narrow beveled front corners w/small carved scrolls, two drawers at the bottom w/leaf-carved pulls, serpentine apron & bracket feet, paneled sides, demountable, original finish, ca. 1850-70, 20 x 54", 8' h. **$3,500**

Glossary

Acanthus: Scalloped leaf decoration. May be applied or carved.

Aesthetic Movement: Furniture style greatly influenced by the Japanese taste, c. 1880-1900. Popular in America, but more prevalent in England.

Anthemion: Carved flat ornament, resembling honeysuckle flower and leaf.

Architectural Mirror: A wall mirror that combines architectural elements of the design period, used to reflect light.

Arrow-Back: Form of chair back from the late Windsor period, identified by a row of flat flaring back stiles that narrow from wider point-type top to slender base.

Art Deco: Furniture style dating from approximately 1925-40.

Art Furniture: Furniture style dating from approximately 1875-1914.

Art Nouveau: Furniture style dating from approximately 1895-1918.

Arts & Crafts: Furniture style dating from approximately 1900-15.

Ball Foot: Turned round foot. Similar to a bun foot, but rounder.

Balloon-Back: Form of chair back shaped like a hot-air balloon, rounded at the top, tapering toward seat.

Baluster: Turned vertical post, with vase or column-form shaped outline.

Banding: Term used to describe edging design.

Barrister Bookcase: A common name for the stacking bookcases with glass fronts, popularized in the Victorian era.

Bellflower: Floral decoration. May be applied or carved.

Bentwood: Term used to describe furniture with an element that was permanently bent through a mechanical process, such as steam or pressure. Well-known designers include Samuel Greeg and Michael Thonet. Other manufacturers of Bentwood furniture were Jacob and Joseph Kohn; Philip Strobel and Son; Sheboygan Chair Co.; and Tidoute Chair Co.

Bergère: Upholstered chair with rounded back, closed arms, and loose seat cushion.

Bird-Cage: Support element of a tilt-top table, generally two blocks separated by columns.

Block: Support element of many furniture forms. Used to increase support or guide drawers, area to apply glue, etc.

Block and Vase: Decorative turning that combines a square and vase element.

Block Foot: Rectangular or square plain feet.

Bootjack Feet: Term used to describe arched foot created by cutting away some of a side or foot board.

Boss, Bosses: Decorative applied ornament(s), often round or oval.

Bow Front: Term used to describe a chest with a slight swell, or bow, in the center.

Box-Stretcher: A structural configuration on the base of a chair that has a bar from leg to leg.

Bracket: Term used to describe curved segment that connects a leg to a seat rail, etc. A bracket can be a functional as well as aesthetic structural segment.

Bracket Foot: One of the simplest of furniture feet, shaped like a bracket, usually with a mitered corner. Variations include a plain bracket foot, a molded bracket foot, or a scrolled bracket foot.

Brasses: Term used to describe metal hardware.

Brass Inlay: Term used to describe technique where thin sheets of different colored brass are laid in a slightly recessed area to create a pattern or design.

Broken Arch Pediment: Term used to describe a triangular or curved pediment that features an open area at the uppermost point.

Bun Foot: Term used to describe a turned foot that features a flattened ball, sometimes on a small square or rectangular shoe or pad.

Butterfly: Term used to describe a shaped element used as a hinge or support.

Button Foot: Term used for small, flattened ball foot.

Butler's Desk: A compartment and writing surface found on some desks and sideboards for use by a servant.

Cabriole Leg: Elegant leg style that curves outward at the knee and tapers inward at the ankle.

Caning: Strips of rattan woven to create a seat or back.

Capital: Top section of a column, used to determine style, usually decorative in form.

Carving: Term used to describe technique that craftsmen used to create designs by using chisels and other implements to sculpt designs.

Case: Term used to describe the box-like body of a piece of furniture, particularly chests, cupboards, or other storage-type pieces of furniture.

Centennial Revival: Furniture style dating from approximately 1875-1915.

Chamfer: Term used to describe a beveled or cut-off corner or edge.

Cheval: A large mirror designed with a base; and can be used in a free-standing position.

Chinoiserie: Decoration featuring American or European interpretation of Oriental motifs.

Chip Carving: An intricate geometric style of carving.

Chippendale: Furniture style dating from approximately 1750-85.

Circa: Common term used to reflect the theory that dates given are approximate and can be a few years early or later than the dates shown, i.e. c., 1850 could be as early as 1845 or as late as 1860.

Classical: Furniture style dating from approximately 1815-1840. Less commonly known as Empire.

Claw and Ball Foot: This style of foot features a carved claw grasping a round ball. Many variations exist, some more detailed than others.

Club Foot: Foot with a slightly pointed toe, usually thick and substantial.

Cockbeaded Molding: Type of molding where a thin beaded edge is the design element.

Colonette: Term used to describe a small column, often an applied type of decoration.

Colonial Revival: Furniture style dating from approximately 1890-1930.

Continuous Arm: Term used to describe an arm that extends from one side to another without breaking for a crest across the back. Commonly found on Windsor chairs, settees, bentwood, and other types of chairs.

Cornice: Top horizontal molding commonly found on case furniture.

Country: Furniture style dating from approximately 1790-1850.

Crestrail: The top rail on the back of a chair.

Cross Stretcher: Base stretcher that intersects another stretcher at right angles, also referred to as X-stretcher.

Cupboard Door: Term used to refer to a simple door created with a flat center section and molded perimeter frame.

Cut-Out Feet: Construction term used to describe a piece of furniture with a solid side piece, where the feet are simply cut out from the side piece.

Dentil Molding: Form of molding that reflects the architectural style of using small rectangles, generally separated by evenly spaced open areas.

Dot-and-Dash Piercing: Type of pierced trim created by alternating circles and sets of horizontal lines.

Dovetails: Joint formed as two pieces of wood are fitted at right angles with interlocking flaring tenons.

Drapery: Carved or inlaid decoration resembling swagged cloth.

Dressing Mirror: A mirror used to view one's appearance, sometimes mounted on a base or used on a table top.

Duncan Phyfe and Phyfe-Types: Furniture style dating from approximately 1795-1840.

Eagle Brasses: Hardware made in the form of a spread-wing eagle, usually made of brass.

Eastlake: Furniture style dating from approximately 1870-1895, part of the Victorian era.

Eglomise: A type of painting on glass where the design is painted on the back and intended to be viewed through the glass, often found as decoration on mirrors.

Egyptian Revival: Furniture style dating from approximately 1870-1890; part of the Victorian era.

Elizabethan Revival: Furniture style dating from approximately 1850-1915; part of the Victorian era.

Empire: Furniture style dating from approximately 1815-40. More commonly known as Classical.

En Suite: Term used to indicate that furniture is a matching part of a set or suite.

Escutcheon: Small decorative brass, metal, or ivory plate used on the outside of a keyhole. Also may be called a "key plate."

Fall Front: Term used to describe a board that lowers from the top to create a writing surface.

Fan Back: Type of Windsor chair back with a rectangular crestrail over a flared, straight-sided back.

Federal: Furniture style dating from approximately 1785-1820.

Festoon: Carved decorative element, sometimes consists of a fruit or floral motif, similar to a drapery.

Finial: Decorative element found as an ornament on top of a case or pediment. Names such as "flame finial" or "corkscrew finial" indicate the three-dimensional shape of the finial.

Fluting: Term used to describe horizontal channel carving.

Foliate: Decoration that resembles leaves. May be applied or carved.

Foot Board: Section of bed frame where user commonly puts feet. Can be paneled, turned, or have elements to support canopy frame.

French Foot: Style of foot with concave curves.

French Restauration: Furniture style dating from

approximately 1830-1850.

Fretwork: Decorative element composed of intersecting lines; can be made with molding or actually cut into the piece.

Gadrooning: Term used to describe swirled or curved fluting, usually an edging.

Gateleg: Extra leg designed to help support table leaf. Support mechanism to attach to table that allows leg to swing freely often resembles a simple gate.

Girandole: A circular convex mirror.

Gothic Revival: Furniture style dating from approximately 1840-90, part of the Victorian era.

Grisalle: Term used to describe painting in tones of gray, usually used on interiors or as a background for other types of decoration.

Graduated Drawers: Term means the drawers that are different in size from one to another; usually the smallest drawer is in the top, the next one slightly larger, etc.

H-Stretcher: A H-configuration of structural rails found on the base of many chairs.

Hairy Paw Foot: Foot carved to depict an animal's hoof with details such as hair and claws found on many examples. Usually wider at the base than the smaller hoof foot.

Hand-Cut Dovetails: Joints made by dovetails that were individually cut by the craftsman. Many are typified by slight inconsistencies in the making.

Head Board: Section of bed frame where user commonly puts head. Can be paneled, turned, or have elements to support canopy frame, often framed by decorative bed hangings.

Hepplewhite: Furniture style dating from approximately 1785-1800.

Hoof Foot: A foot that is carved to resemble an animal's hoof.

Incised Decoration: Term used to describe technique used by craftsmen to create designs, usually lines and geometric shapes, that are not very deeply carved into the wood.

Inlay: Term used to describe technique where thin sheets of different colored woods are laid in a slightly recessed area to create a pattern or design.

Ivory Inlay: Term used to describe technique where thin pieces of ivory are laid in a slightly recessed area to create a pattern or design.

Japanning: Technique using Oriental lacquer work on a wood base, consisting of many layers of varnish and color. Some decorated examples have motifs of figures, animals, and florals that are created in gesso, gilded or silvered, before the lacquer work layers are applied.

Joining: Term used to describe the process of using mortise and tenon joints to create sturdy furniture.

Klismos: Chair form inspired by the ancient Greeks. It is identified by a crestrail, curving uprights, and tapering saber legs. The form was popular in some of the Victorian Revival periods as well as early Classical periods.

Knee Hole Desk: A desk with a flat working surface, usually supported by two banks (or piers) of drawers or legs, allowing the user to sit with their knees under the desk top.

Lady's Desk: Desk of more diminutive proportions, which allowed a lady to sit with her legs under the working surface. Davenport desk: A smaller version of a desk with fold-out working surfaces.

Looking Glass: A term used to describe a small mirror used to view one's image.

Louis XVI Revival: Furniture style dating from approximately 1865-75; part of the Victorian era.

Machine-Cut Dovetails: Joints formed that have consistently even and tight fitting angles. Some later machine-made dovetails are rounded rather than angular.

Marlborough Leg: Style of leg where the leg is square, may be fluted, and generally ends in a blocked foot.

Marquetry: Term used to describe inlay arranged in a specific motif, such as floral or landscapes.

Married: Term used to describe a piece of furniture where the top and base were combined, sometimes bridging two generations or different time frames.

Medallion: Round, oval, or spherical ornament, usually applied.

Mission, Prairie: Furniture style dating from approximately 1900-15.

Modernism-Era: Furniture style dating from approximately 1940 to 1960.

Modernism Era, Pop: Furniture style dating from approximately 1945-70.

Molded Bracket Foot: Bracket foot with additional molding as a decorative element on the foot or at the connection with the case.

Molding: Decorative piece of wood used for ornamental purposes.

Mortise and Tenon Joint: Joint created when the tenon, a small tab-like extension, is fitted into a square or rectangular opening, known as a mortise. Sometimes a mortise and tenon joint has a wooden peg to securely fasten the joint. When a mortise and tenon joint is visible to the viewer, it is called an "exposed mortise and tenon."

Naturalistic Revival: Furniture style dating from approximately 1850-1914; part of the Victorian era.

Neoclassic or Greco-Roman: Furniture style dating from approximately 1790-1815.

Neo-Greek Revival: Furniture style dating from approximately 1855-1885; part of the Victorian era.

Ogee: Term used to describe a molding shaped like the letter "S." Also called a cyma curve.

Ormolu Mount: Term used to describe the technique where gilt-covered metal mountings are used as decorative or functional elements.

Overlapping Drawer: Term indicating a slight extension on the face of the drawer that covers the drawer opening tightly when closed, thus overlapping the case.

Over Mantel Mirror: A term used to describe large mirrors used over a fireplace mantel, primarily used to reflect light into a room.

Over-Upholstered: Upholstered section that appears to be overstuffed.

Oxbow Front: Another name for a reverse serpentine-shaped front.

Pad Foot: Term used to describe a small rounded foot that rests on a platform or small base.

Palmette: Decorative carving in the shape of a palm leaf or fan.

Patera: Term used to describe an oval or round motif with segments that radiate from the center.

Pediment: Uppermost section of a case style of furniture.

Period Brasses: Term used to describe hardware that is original to the piece, usually used only when the hardware is made of brass, but sometimes this phrase is used to denote any period metal hardware.

Period Hardware: Term used to describe hardware that is original to the piece, dating from the time of manufacturing.

Piecrust Edge: Term used to describe edge of a circular form that resembles the edge of a pie.

Pier Mirror: A large mirror either hung over a pier table or hung at a level so one could view skirts and feet.

Pilaster: Column with a flat or rectangular side, used for ornamental purposes only.

Plinth: Term used to describe base of column.

Queen Anne: Furniture style dating from approximately 1720-50.

Reeding: Term used to describe vertical channel carving.

Replaced Hardware: Term used to describe hardware

that is not original to the piece. May not be stylistically accurate.

Reproduction Hardware: Term used to describe hardware made to look like antique or period hardware.

Restauration: Term used to describe a predominately French furniture style dated about 1830-50. It features simple lines and light woods.

Renaissance Revival: Furniture style dating from approximately 1860-85; part of the Victorian era.

Ring Turning: Term used to describe molding or legs turned on a lathe, with small rings as part of the design element.

Rococo Revival: Furniture style dating from approximately 1845-1870; part of the Victorian era.

Roll Top: Type of somewhat flexible closure used to close a desk where a sliding section moves up and behind the fitted interior of the desk. Usually made like a tambour, but often of large dimensioned wood and consequently can be more rigid than a standard tambour.

Rosette: Rose-like round ornament, sometimes divided into small segments or petals.

Saber Leg: Type of chair leg that tapers and curves. Shape resembles a cavalry saber.

Sack Back: Type of Windsor chair where the back is rounded.

Saddle Seat: Type of seat where wood is carved to gently fit user comfortably.

Scallop: Term used to describe decorative carved or applied element that resembles a shell.

Scroll: Decorative element consisting of swirls.

Scrolled Bracket Foot: Bracket foot with a scrolled design at the sides.

Scroll Mirror: A scrolled mirror frame, made to be hung on a wall.

Secondary Wood: Term that refers to the wood used on the interior of drawers, perhaps the back, or areas that are unseen.

Secretaire a'abattant: French term used to describe a secretary, especially those with detailed interiors.

Secretary: Term used to describe a desk with a high bookcase top.

Serpentine Front: Term used to describe a more shaped top, often having several curves.

Shaker: Furniture style dating from approximately 1800-1914.

Shaving Mirror: A small tabletop mirror, used to view one's appearance while shaving. Usually found on bases, sometimes with small drawers to hold accessories.

Shell Carving: Term used to describe decorative carved elements that resemble shells or scallops.

Sheraton: Furniture style dating from approximately 1800-20.

Side Rail: Chair side rails extending from the crestrail to seat.

Six-Board Construction: Term used to describe a blanket chest made from six boards, one for the top, front, back, bottom, and sides.

Skirt: Connective piece often found between table legs and table top. May be scalloped or plain or contain a drawer opening.

Slant Front: Term that describes a flat writing surface that folds down from the top to a comfortable writing height. Also known as a slant lid.

Slant Lid: Term that describes a flat writing surface that folds down from the top to a comfortable writing height. Also known as a slant front.

Snake Foot: Term used to describe a small rounded foot, often carved with eyes or other reptile-like details.

Spade Foot: Term used to describe small trowel-shaped foot.

Spanish Foot: Term used to describe sweeping carved scrolling foot.

Spindle: Turned rod used as a support element in chairs, birdcage supports, etc.

Spool Turning: Term used to describe turned element where lathe is used and end result is a series of spools or rounded elements.

Stretcher Base: The structural members that extend from chair leg to chair leg, adding stability.

Stringing: Term used to describe inlaid wood that is usually lighter than base wood. Can be found used either horizontally or vertically.

Swag: Decoration similar to drapery or festoon, to give the illusion of draped fabric.

Tambour: Technique whereby thin strips of wood are glued to a cloth backing, retaining some flexibility. Frequently used as doors or other types of enclosures.

Teardrop: Type of hardware shaped like a pendant, usually with a brass or metal backplate and turned wooden teardrop.

Tester: Term used to describe bed frame with a canopy.

Thumb-Molded: Type of molding where edge is smooth, as though a thumb has carefully smoothed out the edges.

Trifid Foot: Delicate foot that is carved to resemble three toes.

Vasiform Splat: A decorative splat, usually found on chairs, shaped like a vase.

Veneer: Thin layer of wood glued to less expensive wood base.

Victorian: Furniture style dating from approximately 1840-90, contains many sub-styles.

Wall Mirror: A mirror designed to be hung on the wall and used for either viewing of one's image or reflecting light.

William and Mary: Furniture style dating from approximately 1685-1720.

Windsor: Furniture style dating from approximately 1750 to present.

X-Stretcher: A type of chair base configuration that has elements that go across the base and the stretcher bars cross, sometimes joined together. Also referred to as a cross-stretcher.